THE OFFICIAL
**ENGLAND**
EURO 2004 BOOK

CARLTON
BOOKS

# THE OFFICIAL ENGLAND EURO 2004 BOOK

THIS IS A CARLTON BOOK



The views expressed are not The FA's

This edition published in 2004 by Carlton Books Limited, 20 Mortimer Street, London W1N 7RD

ISBN 1 84442 864 8



A CIP catalogue for this book is available from the British Library.



**Editorial Manager** Martin Corteel
**Executive Editor** Roland Hall
**Writers** Jim Drewett, Rob Wightman, Sam Pilger
**Production** Lisa French
**Project Art Direction** Darren Jordan
**Design** Paul Sinclair at Parallax Studios
**Picture Research** Stephen O'Kelly

Printed and bound in Portugal

ENGLAND

# CONTENTS

## Welcome!

**Hello and welcome to The Official England Euro 2004 Book...**

It has been a long and difficult journey to reach Portugal 2004, but we made it in the end. After rather a slow start, we gained momentum and I think we deserved to win an automatic place in the finals. I was particularly proud of the way the players performed in our final match against Turkey in Istanbul. They showed their character and pride in playing for their country and produced a really marvellous performance to gain the one point we needed.

Now we can look ahead and prepare for the finals. Hopefully we can build on the experience of World Cup 2002 where we reached the quarter-finals. We still maintain the core of that team and some more excellent young players have come through to give me some nice selection problems too! I think we have a good chance of winning the tournament and you can be sure everyone involved in the England set-up will be doing everything we can try and achieve that. Your support has been invaluable throughout the qualifiers and whether you are watching at home or come out to Portugal I hope we can give you lots more reasons to cheer this summer.

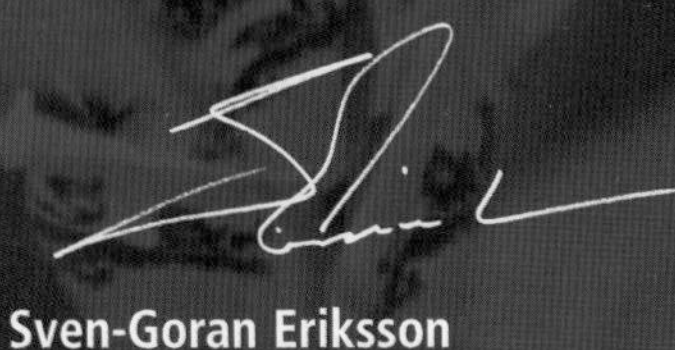

**Sven-Goran Eriksson**

74
26
63
50
28
66
56
30

# PORTUGAL BOUND

**Six wins, two draws and no defeats – England's qualifying stats sound pretty impressive. But reaching Euro 2004 wasn't all smooth sailing...**

12 OCTOBER 2002, BRATISLAVA

## SLOVAKIA 1 ENGLAND 2

NEMETH 23 — BECKHAM 64, OWEN 82

THERE WAS RAIN, RAIN AND MORE rain as England prepared for their first qualifier. For almost two days it didn't let up in Bratislava. The heavens opened and then refused to close, to such an extent there were some doubts about whether the game would be played at all. It was, but the sodden pitch proved a real problem for both sides.

The hosts in particular were soon cursing the inclement weather when Vittek wriggled clear through on six minutes but the ball stubbornly refused to sit up as he tried to get his shot away.

England tried to settle after this early escape but Slovakia weren't helping, surging forward at every opportunity as 30,000 fanatical fans bellowed their support in the biggest game in Slovakia's short history.

They had good reason to cheer in the 23rd minute when the English-based Szilard Nemeth struck a firm shot past David Seaman to give Slovakia the lead.

Half an hour of frantic attempted recovery followed as England created – and failed to take – chance after chance. The crowd, sensing a historic victory, began doing a Mexican wave. One David Beckham free-kick later, the waves had subsided. The England skipper curled one in from 35 yards, Michael Owen poked out a toe. It didn't connect but it was enough to put off the keeper and the ball bounced into the corner of the net.

From 1–1 England grew stronger, pushing for a winner. It came with eight minutes remaining. Scholes crossed and this time Owen did connect, nudging the ball home at the near post.

England had started the campaign with a vital away victory.

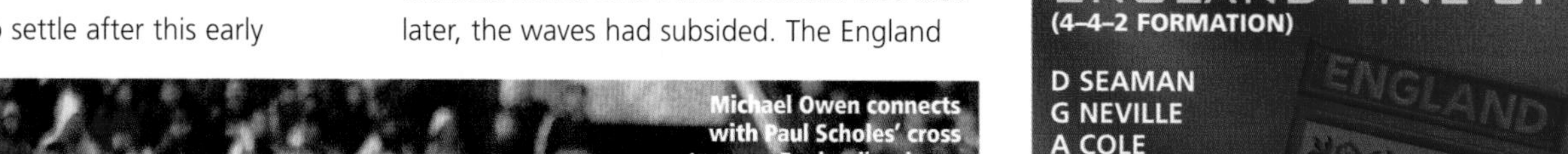

Michael Owen connects with Paul Scholes' cross to score England's winner in Bratislava.

### ENGLAND LINE-UP
**(4-4-2 FORMATION)**

D SEAMAN
G NEVILLE
A COLE
G SOUTHGATE
J WOODGATE
D BECKHAM
N BUTT
S GERRARD (K DYER, 77)
P SCHOLES
E HESKEY (A SMITH, 90)
M OWEN (O HARGREAVES, 86)

SUBS NOT USED D JAMES, D MILLS, U EHIOGU, D VASSELL

BOOKED S GERRARD (42), P SCHOLES (68)

| | P | W | D | L | F | A | GD | Pts |
|---|---|---|---|---|---|---|---|---|
| TURKEY | 2 | 2 | 0 | 0 | 5 | 1 | +4 | 6 |
| **ENGLAND** | **1** | **1** | **0** | **0** | **2** | **1** | **+1** | **3** |
| LIECH'STEIN | 1 | 0 | 1 | 0 | 1 | 1 | 0 | 1 |
| MACEDONIA | 2 | 0 | 1 | 1 | 2 | 3 | -1 | 1 |
| SLOVAKIA | 2 | 0 | 0 | 2 | 1 | 5 | -4 | 0 |

2–2: Gerrard celebrates his thunderbolt equaliser.

16 OCTOBER 2002, ST MARY'S STADIUM, SOUTHAMPTON

# ENGLAND 2 MACEDONIA 2

BECKHAM 13, GERRARD 35 — SAKIRI 10, TRAJANOV 24

FOUR DAYS AFTER THE COMEBACK against Slovakia, the England players were back in the UK and soon in familiar territory on the pitch as they found themselves a goal behind again! This time it was the spirited Macedonians taking the lead courtesy of Artim Sakiri, who silenced the St Mary's Stadium with a 10th minute corner that swirled its way into the top corner of the net before David Seaman could react.

To their credit, England responded almost immediately, Paul Scholes turning provider once more as he chipped forward into the path of David Beckham's incisive dash through the centre. The skipper controlled the ball smartly with his chest before coolly chipping it over the advancing Milosevski.

Any spectator developing a theory that England were making a habit of coming back from conceded goals had further confirmation over the next 25 minutes.

A fairly innocuous low ball was played into the England penalty area but Sol Campbell's clearance only reached Trajanov who was lurking on the edge of the area. The midfielder found the perfect finish to curl the ball past Seaman. Not for the first time, the stadium went quiet. England fans weren't encouraged to get too vocal either as the home side appeared to be having one of those nights. Scholes electing to pass to Owen when he should have shot, Beckham choosing to shoot when he should have put Michael Owen in and then Scholes blasting over after Beckham had expertly set him up.

Fortunately there was only one thought in Steven Gerrard's mind when the ball reached him on the edge of the area in the 35th minute. He took one touch before smashing the ball almost through the net. England were back on level terms. Yet again.

This time however there was to be no late winner. Macedonia's second half display of resilience and speed on the break ensured a lively but ultimately goalless last 45 minutes.

A frustrated England had to settle for a home draw. Not the ideal result but not a disaster either.

## ENGLAND LINE-UP
**(4-4-2 FORMATION)**

D SEAMAN
G NEVILLE
A COLE
J WOODGATE
S CAMPBELL
D BECKHAM
S GERRARD (N BUTT, 56)
P SCHOLES
W BRIDGE (D VASSELL, 58)
A SMITH
M OWEN

SUBS NOT USED
D MILLS, D JAMES, G SOUTHGATE
O HARGREAVES, F LAMPARD

BOOKED D BECKHAM (40),
A SMITH (SENT OFF, 90)

| | P | W | D | L | F | A | GD | Pts |
|---|---|---|---|---|---|---|---|---|
| TURKEY | 3 | 3 | 0 | 0 | 10 | 1 | +9 | 9 |
| **ENGLAND** | **2** | **1** | **1** | **0** | **4** | **3** | **+1** | **4** |
| MACEDONIA | 3 | 0 | 2 | 1 | 4 | 5 | -1 | 2 |
| LIECH'STEIN | 2 | 0 | 1 | 1 | 1 | 6 | -5 | 1 |
| SLOVAKIA | 2 | 0 | 0 | 2 | 1 | 5 | -4 | 0 |

29 MARCH 2003, VADUZ

# LIECH'STEIN 0 ENGLAND 2

OWEN 28, BECKHAM 53

Owen powers home his 20th goal from 36 international starts.

NO FRILLS, COMEBACKS OR unnecessary drama required. England arrived in Vaduz knowing that in qualifiers the result is all. With Turkey to come in four days, a tidy performance and three points would do nicely here. And that's what Sven's team delivered.

The visitors began well and were perhaps a little unfortunate not to score sooner with David Beckham, Kieron Dyer and Gary Neville all pushing forward. But on 28 minutes the breakthrough finally came. Beckham's pass released Emile Heskey on the right and the striker's powerful run ended with a sharp cross that Michael Owen smartly headed in from six yards. It was Owen's 20th international goal, from just 36 starts. The doubters who once questioned his form were again left to shuffle uncomfortably in their seats.

The second goal took a while in coming. England dominated, with Beckham and Heskey both going close, but it took a free-kick from the captain to seal the victory. Some 25 yards out, the familiar run up and curling strike ended with the equally familiar sight of the ball in the back of the net. Jehle, the Liechtenstein keeper, may have known what was coming but could still do nothing to prevent it happening. It must be pretty frustrating for every keeper who stands behind his wall watching Beckham line the ball up, knowing that if he hits it right there's really not a lot you can do about it.

With the result secured, Sven substituted Beckham and Steven Gerrard, no doubt expecting more demands to be made of them against Turkey later in the week.

## ENGLAND LINE-UP

**(4-4-2 FORMATION)**

D JAMES
G NEVILLE
W BRIDGE
R FERDINAND
G SOUTHGATE
D BECKHAM (D MURPHY, 70)
P SCHOLES
S GERRARD (N BUTT, 66)
K DYER
E HESKEY (W ROONEY, 80)
M OWEN

SUBS NOT USED
P ROBINSON, D MILLS, D VASSELL, J WOODGATE

BOOKED NO-ONE

| | P | W | D | L | F | A | GD | Pts |
|---|---|---|---|---|---|---|---|---|
| TURKEY | 3 | 3 | 0 | 0 | 10 | 1 | +9 | 9 |
| **ENGLAND** | **3** | **2** | **1** | **0** | **6** | **3** | **+3** | **7** |
| SLOVAKIA | 3 | 1 | 0 | 2 | 3 | 5 | -2 | 3 |
| MACEDONIA | 4 | 0 | 2 | 2 | 4 | 7 | -3 | 2 |
| LIECH'STEIN | 3 | 0 | 1 | 2 | 1 | 8 | -7 | 1 |

DIAMONDS MAY BE A GIRL'S BEST friend, but Turkey weren't enamoured this evening. Sven's decision to use a new diamond formation, and his selection of Wayne Rooney from the start both paid off for the England manager, even if his side left it late to make their breakthrough.

All week the match had been hyped up in the media and by kick-off you could sense both teams were raring to go. The game was physical right from the start and both Rooney – obviously enjoying his first start – and Beckham both came close to scoring. Rooney had seen his goal-bound effort blocked on the line and the fired-up skipper tried to smash the ball home but scuffed his shot wide.

Turkey weren't afraid to push forward either. On the half hour Basturk found space to unleash a venomous drive that David James did well both to parry and to be first to the rebound.

But it was Rooney who caught the eye. Twice in the space of a couple of minutes his power and skill rocked the Turks to create chances Owen uncharacteristically failed to put away.

The second half saw England step up a gear in search of that elusive goal. The injured Owen made way for Darius Vassell and the Aston Villa striker was quickly in the thick of things. He brought a fine save from Rustu in the Turkish goal within minutes of coming on and then forced a corner that was to prove decisive.

Beckham's kick was only partially cleared to Wayne Bridge who set up Rio Ferdinand at the far post. His effort was saved but Vassell was there to snap up the rebound with a low drive into the net. The mixture of glee and relief on Sven's face told its own story. Everyone in the ground knew the importance of the goal.

As Turkey chased an equaliser, opportunities opened up for both sides. James made an excellent save to keep Nihat out in the 81st minute and then the pace of Kieron Dyer, on for Rooney, proved too much for Ergun. The Turkish number six tugged Dyer's shirt in desperation and the referee immediately pointed to the penalty spot. Beckham tucked the kick away and England had six points from two games. A good few days' work.

**ENGLAND LINE-UP**
**(4-1-3-1-1 FORMATION)**

D JAMES
G NEVILLE
W BRIDGE
R FERDINAND
S GERRARD
S CAMPBELL
N BUTT
D BECKHAM
P SCHOLES
W ROONEY (K DYER, 89)
M OWEN (D VASSELL, 58)

**SUBS NOT USED**
P ROBINSON, D MILLS, F LAMPARD, J WOODGATE, E HESKEY

**BOOKED**
D BECKHAM (9)
R FERDINAND (90)

| | P | W | D | L | F | A | GD | Pts |
|---|---|---|---|---|---|---|---|---|
| **ENGLAND** | **4** | **3** | **1** | **0** | **8** | **3** | **+5** | **10** |
| TURKEY | 4 | 3 | 0 | 1 | 10 | 3 | +7 | 9 |
| SLOVAKIA | 4 | 2 | 0 | 2 | 7 | 5 | +2 | 6 |
| MACEDONIA | 4 | 0 | 2 | 2 | 4 | 7 | -3 | 2 |
| LIECH'STEIN | 4 | 0 | 1 | 3 | 1 | 12 | -11 | 1 |

2 APRIL 2003, STADIUM OF LIGHT, SUNDERLAND

# ENGLAND 2 TURKEY 0

VASSELL 75, BECKHAM (PEN) 90

**Substitute Darius Vassell came on and gave England new impetus.**

**11 JUNE 2003, RIVERSIDE STADIUM, MIDDLESBROUGH**

# ENGLAND 2 SLOVAKIA 1

OWEN 60 (PEN), 72 JANOCKO 31

OLD HABITS DIE HARD. ONCE AGAIN England conceded the first goal. Fortunately, once again they revived to make an impressive comeback.

Things started well enough. With news filtering through that Macedonia were leading Turkey and bright sunshine warming the Riverside Stadium, there was a sense of optimism spreading through the stadium. Almost from kick-off Steven Gerrard slid though an inch-perfect ball for Michael Owen to take in his stride. The striker unleashed a smart effort that Slovakia keeper Konig did well to keep out.

So far, so good. But as Slovakia settled into their stride, England's defence seemed to come undone. Every time the visitors pushed forward, the hosts were at sixes and sevens. On more than one occasion only poor finishing kept Slovakia from taking the lead as they began to dominate proceedings. A goal seemed inevitable, although the manner in which it eventually came was somewhat unexpected.

Janocko curled in one of those angled free-kicks that cause trouble for any defence. As the ball bent towards the goal, a clutch of players tried to get a touch but it eluded everyone, including David James, and slipped into the far corner of the net.

It could have been worse. Within minutes both Demo and Nemeth wasted clear-cut chances to grab a second goal while England struggled to find defensive cohesion.

Something needed to change and Sven wisely acted, withdrawing Danny Mills from the action and reverting to a conventional four-man midfield.

The second half saw the benefits of the tinkering. England looked a different side, as defensive dithering was replaced with attacking intent that the Slovaks couldn't match.

At the forefront was Owen, who pushed forward at every opportunity. On the hour, he weaved past three players and was goal-bound when he was squeezed out by two Slovakian defenders. The referee pointed to the spot and Owen coolly dispatched the penalty, artfully waiting for Konig to commit before rolling the ball past him. Twelve minutes later he secured the victory, heading home from Steven Gerrard's cross.

England's tendency to concede a goal before rallying was hardly ideal but winning matches was still a habit worth continuing.

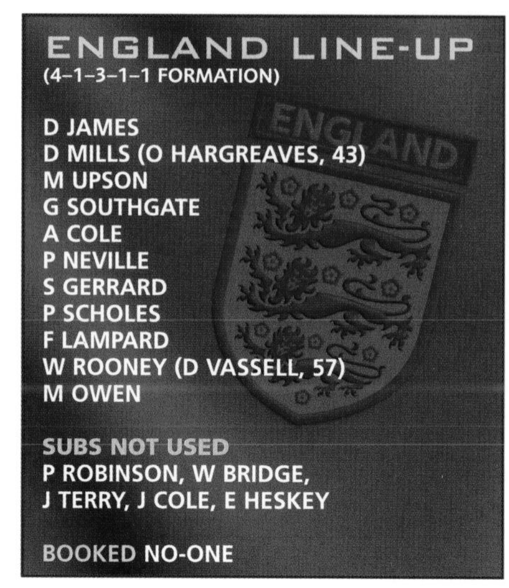

## ENGLAND LINE-UP
**(4-1-3-1-1 FORMATION)**

D JAMES
D MILLS (O HARGREAVES, 43)
M UPSON
G SOUTHGATE
A COLE
P NEVILLE
S GERRARD
P SCHOLES
F LAMPARD
W ROONEY (D VASSELL, 57)
M OWEN

SUBS NOT USED
P ROBINSON, W BRIDGE, J TERRY, J COLE, E HESKEY

BOOKED NO-ONE

| | P | W | D | L | F | A | GD | Pts |
|---|---|---|---|---|---|---|---|---|
| TURKEY | 6 | 5 | 0 | 1 | 14 | 5 | +9 | 15 |
| **ENGLAND** | **5** | **4** | **1** | **0** | **10** | **4** | **+6** | **13** |
| SLOVAKIA | 6 | 2 | 0 | 4 | 8 | 8 | 0 | 6 |
| MACEDONIA | 6 | 1 | 2 | 3 | 9 | 11 | -2 | 5 |
| LIECH'STEIN | 5 | 0 | 1 | 4 | 2 | 15 | -13 | 1 |

**Guess who's just scored again…?**

At the age of 17 years and 317 days, Wayne Rooney becomes England's youngest-ever goalscorer.

6 SEPTEMBER 2003, SKOPJE

# MACEDONIA 1 ENGLAND 2

HRISTOV 26 ROONEY 53, BECKHAM (PEN) 61

ANOTHER GAME, ANOTHER comeback. We knew the script by now, so when Hristov gave Macedonia the lead after 26 minutes, it was clear there was still a long way to go.

When the England scouts had reported back from watching Macedonia, they warned that the hosts would start quickly and brightly and they were proved entirely correct. With the home crowd roaring them on (and some Macedonian supporters burning an England flag) the passion of the crowd was palpable and Dragi Kanatlarovski's side responded with confidence and purpose.

Artim Sakiri, England's chief tormentor at St Mary's last year, looked to be in the sort of form to cause England problems once again while David Beckham's every touch was being booed by the exciteable Macedonian public.

Sol Campbell was kept at full stretch by some good attacking play from the hosts but he was unable to cut out Grozdanovski's cross from the right. David James kept out Pandev's initial effort but Hristov was there to tuck home the rebound.

Try as they might, England couldn't find a response and went in at the interval still behind. It was time for another of Sven's tactical changes. He took off Frank Lampard, moved Owen Hargreaves into the centre and sent on Emile Heskey to make an attacking 4–3–3 for the second half. The reward was almost immediate.

Eight minutes after the restart Beckham picked out Heskey with a chipped ball and the Liverpool striker directed a header into Wayne Rooney's path. Rooney moved smoothly onto the ball before firing home a dazzling half-volley from the edge of the area. The goal gave Rooney a place in the history books as England's youngest-ever goalscorer.

At 1–1, England were in the ascendancy and the winner wasn't long in coming. Beckham lifted a free-kick towards John Terry whose quick turn was too much for Zezuz. The clumsy tackle that followed gave Beckham a chance from the penalty spot. He converted for his 12th goal in 25 starts under Sven.

The hosts refused to concede the result and continued to push forward in search of an equaliser but Campbell stood firm, dealing calmly with everything that came his way.

This result made it four qualifying wins in a row for England. Victory on Wednesday at Old Trafford against Liechtenstein would ensure that only a point would be required in Istanbul. Despite the drama, things were shaping up nicely.

## ENGLAND LINE-UP
**(4–4–2 FORMATION)**

D JAMES
G NEVILLE
J TERRY
S CAMPBELL
A COLE
D BECKHAM
F LAMPARD (E HESKEY 46)
N BUTT
O HARGREAVES
W ROONEY (P NEVILLE 75)
M OWEN (K DYER 85)
E HESKEY

SUBS NOT USED
P ROBINSON, M UPSON, W BRIDGE, J COLE

BOOKED S CAMPBELL (24)
D BECKHAM (42)

| | P | W | D | L | F | A | GD | Pts |
|---|---|---|---|---|---|---|---|---|
| TURKEY | 7 | 6 | 0 | 1 | 17 | 5 | +12 | 18 |
| **ENGLAND** | **6** | **5** | **1** | **0** | **12** | **5** | **+7** | **16** |
| SLOVAKIA | 6 | 2 | 0 | 4 | 8 | 8 | 0 | 6 |
| MACEDONIA | 7 | 1 | 2 | 4 | 10 | 13 | -3 | 5 |
| LIECH'STEIN | 6 | 0 | 1 | 5 | 2 | 18 | -16 | 1 |

10 SEPTEMBER 2003, OLD TRAFFORD, MANCHESTER

# ENGLAND 2 LIECHTENSTEIN 0

OWEN 46, ROONEY 52

Rooney strikes again!

SVEN KNEW THAT A WIN WOULD ensure England had one foot in Euro 2004 and he sent out a team that would chase a victory, with the three-pronged attack of James Beattie, Wayne Rooney and Michael Owen.

Beattie promptly hit the bar with a thunderous left-foot strike, quickly followed by Owen almost punishing a fumble by Jehle. But it was Rooney who looked the biggest threat. The youngest player on the pitch, he already displayed the assurance of a veteran international. His weaving runs and smart passing had the visitors wrong-footed for 45 minutes. All that was missing was a goal. In their now customary style, England were saving their best for the second half.

Within a minute of the restart the hosts were ahead. A whipped-in cross from Steven Gerrard was met by the head of Owen and England were on their way. The second goal came six minutes later

Owen drove the ball out wide to David Beckham who picked out Gerrard's run to the far post. The Liverpool midfielder placed a perfect header into the path of Rooney and the youngster made no mistake with a powerful strike. The reaction of the crowd made it clear that they had a new hero.

Within minutes, Sven had taken Gerrard and Beckham off and thoughts were already turning to the following month's final qualifier. Thanks to Rooney and co, a point against Turkey would be enough to qualify.

ENGLAND LINE-UP
**(4–3–3 FORMATION)**

**D JAMES**
**G NEVILLE**
**M UPSON**
**W BRIDGE**
**J TERRY**
**D BECKHAM (O HARGREAVES, 55)**
**S GERRARD (P NEVIILLE, 55)**
**F LAMPARD**
**W ROONEY (J COLE, 69)**
**M OWEN**
**J BEATTIE**

**SUBS NOT USED**
**P ROBINSON, S CAMPBELL,**
**K DYER, E HESKEY**

**BOOKED W BRIDGE (56)**

| | P | W | D | L | F | A | GD | Pts |
|---|---|---|---|---|---|---|---|---|
| **ENGLAND** | **7** | **6** | **1** | **0** | **14** | **5** | **+9** | **19** |
| TURKEY | 7 | 6 | 0 | 1 | 17 | 5 | +12 | 18 |
| SLOVAKIA | 7 | 2 | 1 | 4 | 9 | 9 | 0 | 7 |
| MACEDONIA | 8 | 1 | 3 | 4 | 11 | 14 | -3 | 6 |
| LIECH'STEIN | 7 | 0 | 1 | 6 | 2 | 20 | -18 | 1 |

IT WAS NEVER GOING TO BE EASY FOR England to travel to Istanbul to get a result. But from the tense atmosphere within the Sükrü Saraçoglu Stadium it soon became apparent that the Turkish team would also feel the pressure of trying to deliver.

In fact it was the hosts who seemed more stifled by the occasion (and their fans) as England got off to a good start, playing smart and pacey football. Nicky Butt's short, accurate passing provided a good foundation from which to build attacking moves, and the quality of Paul Scholes, Steven Gerrard and

ENGLAND LINE-UP
**(4–4–2 FORMATION)**

**D JAMES**
**G NEVILLE**
**A COLE**
**S CAMPBELL**
**J TERRY**
**S GERRARD**
**N BUTT**
**D BECKHAM**
**P SCHOLES (F LAMPARD, 88)**
**E HESKEY (D VASSELL, 67)**
**W ROONEY (K DYER, 71)**

**SUBS NOT USED**
**P NEVILLE, P ROBINSON,**
**M UPSON, W BRIDGE**

**BOOKED N BUTT (80)**

**GROUP 7 FINAL TABLE**

| | P | W | D | L | F | A | GD | Pts |
|---|---|---|---|---|---|---|---|---|
| **ENGLAND** | **8** | **6** | **2** | **0** | **14** | **5** | **+9** | **20** |
| TURKEY | 8 | 6 | 1 | 1 | 17 | 5 | +12 | 19 |
| SLOVAKIA | 8 | 3 | 1 | 4 | 11 | 9 | +2 | 10 |
| MACEDONIA | 8 | 1 | 3 | 4 | 11 | 14 | -3 | 6 |
| LIECH'STEIN | 8 | 0 | 1 | 7 | 2 | 22 | -20 | 1 |

**All hands to the pump – England only needed a draw to qualify.**

David Beckham ensured the visitors looked comfortable in possession.

For the Turks, Nihat was the main threat. An acrobatic volley and a 35-yard free-kick both tested James in the first half. Although the real drama of the half took place in the Turkish penalty box.

A slinky run by Gerrard came to an abrupt halt when he was fouled, and the referee pointed to the spot. As Beckham stepped up, the European Championship finals appeared to be beckoning. But as the skipper went to strike the ball his left foot gave way on the slippery surface and his mis-hit shot flew over the bar.

It could have proved the pivotal moment. The crowd's cheers intensified, re-igniting the home side. Instead, England kept their heads and impressively retained control of the match.

The second half was as fierce as the first as the pressure on Turkey to get a result increased. John Terry and Sol Campbell remained resolute in defence, Beckham had a goal ruled out for offside and Nihat almost snatched a late winner. But when the final whistle blew, England had earned the point we needed. Portugal, here we come!

11 OCTOBER 2003, ISTANBUL

## TURKEY 0 ENGLAND 0

# OBECKHAM

**Honoured by the Queen for his services to football last November, David Beckham OBE is now aiming to lead England to glory at Euro 2004 this summer**

David Beckham doesn't really have quiet years. The most famous footballer in the world is rather too high profile for such luxuries. But even by his standards the last 12 months have been somewhat eventful.

There was the intense and continual speculation concerning his future at the club he'd supported all his life. His subsequent departure from Manchester United for a new life in Spain at Real Madrid. A summer tour of the Far East that seemed to involve almost as many press trailing around as locals. Oh, and there was the small matter of leading his country through a successful campaign to reach the 2004 European Championship.

As per usual, David has handled everything with aplomb. A fact that was recognised by none other than Her Majesty the Queen last November, when he received his OBE.

"Victoria is so proud," beamed David at Buckingham Palace. "She might even have had a little cry. And I'm so proud that she could be here today to share this with me. This is an amazing day, a dream come true. It's definitely on a par with my football medals – if not better.

"Her Majesty asked if it was exhausting travelling around the world playing football matches. I said no, because I'm used to it now. I know Her Majesty is a football fan because when I was at a Number 10 reception, the Prime Minister told me he had watched a World Cup game on television with the Queen and William and Harry."

Presumably the royals will be watching a few more matches this summer, when the events of the last year will have become mere footnotes in an already extraordinary career.

David himself has been remarkably candid on all that has gone on.

"It was quite a few days" is his understated take on the week leading up to the Turkey match in Istanbul. "But the performance we put in on the night was the best possible way for it to end. To a man, I thought the team were magnificent. Against a very good side, in an intimidating atmosphere, and with no fans there to support us, we really showed what we are capable of as a team. I was very proud to be captain of England that night.

**"If we can peak at the right time in Portugal, we know we need fear no-one. I think few teams will relish playing us."**

"The huddle the team went into at the end wasn't planned but it said everything about our unity and our desire to succeed. Our objective now has got to be to keep that level of performance and team spirit going. If we can peak at the right time in Portugal, we know we need fear no-one. I think few teams will relish playing us."

One thing is evident when you listen to the England skipper these days. He has grown into his responsibilities as the national team's leader and despite constant attention and pressure, he still manages to perform at the highest level seemingly undistracted. No longer in the bosom of a club who nurtured him from youth, he still gets on with the job at hand.

"I have very good memories of my time at Manchester United," he says. "They were very happy times. But now I am a Real Madrid player. I have joined a great squad with extraordinary players. People expect a lot from us and rightly so. I hope I become a better player day after day. That's one of my goals. I want to improve in every situation."

Despite all he's achieved, it's clear David harbours further ambitions:

"I've been voted the second best player in the world twice," he says with a smile. "One day I'd like to become the best. Playing my club football in Spain has given me a new lease of life and I hope I can carry that into Euro 2004."

A happy – and still hungry – Beckham is good news for England fans, for David is justly famous around the world for his stunning sporting ability.

"I'm really enjoying my time with Real Madrid and I've settled in well but I always look forward to playing for my country. Like any footballer, I always get excited at the thought of playing in big competitions and this summer will be no exception. At the end of the day I'm a footballer. And that's what it's all about. The football."

Beckham will be one of the most watched players in Portugal in the summer, as he tries to add the European Championship to his already impressive football CV. Few players in the world have the ability (or energy!) to change the outcome of a game as he can.

## THIERRY HENRY | FRANCE

"Henry has got so much pace it is frightening, he really is incredible – he could sell pace he has so much! He also scores goals and if you give him half a yard he's gone and you will be in trouble.

"He first really made an impression when he came to Arsenal, but I knew of him when he was at Juventus. Looking back it is amazing that they sold him."

# ENGLAND in EUROPE a brief history

**England have always struggled to make an impact in the European Championship. Maybe, it's about time we won it then...**

ENGLAND OPTED NOT TO TAKE PART IN the inaugural European Nations Cup (as it was first known) hosted by France in 1960 and won by the USSR. The original format saw the early rounds played over two legs, on a knock-out basis, until the semi-final stage, which took place in a host country.

### First-time flop

England entered the qualifying stages for the second Championship, to be held in Spain in 1964, only to fall to France at the first hurdle. In Spain, the USSR made a robust defence of the title, only to lose a hard-fought final 2–1 to the host nation.

### Italian triumph

England's next European adventure was as world champions and we qualified for our first finals. In June 1968, Yugoslavia stood between England and a place in the final against the USSR or host nation Italy. But while Italy survived to win through on the toss of a coin, England slumped to a 0–1 reverse. The Italians triumphed in the replayed final, winning 2–0 after a drawn first match.

### Germany on top

Four years later West Germany were crowned European champions in Belgium, after comprehensively beating the Soviet Union in the final. England failed to reach the finals after falling to the Germans in the quarter-finals.

It all went wrong for England against a classy Holland side during the 1988 European Championship.

### Czechs win shoot-out

Yugoslavia hosted the 1976 tournament, but again England were unable to make the cut. Czechoslovakia triumphed over West Germany on penalties in an absorbing final which saw the defending champions force extra-time after being two goals down.

### Favourite falls

England arrived in Italy for the 1980 tournament as one of the favourites. An excellent strike by Ray Wilkins saw Ron Greenwood's men make the perfect start against Belgium on 12 June. But the impressive Belgians equalised through Jan Ceulemans to claim a draw.

Three days later England faced Italy in a must-win encounter. But Italy's Marco Tardelli took advantage of England's sloppy defending to grab the only goal of the game. Goals from Trevor Brooking and Tony Woodcock secured victory over Spain in England's final match but Greenwood's men were still eliminated. Ultimately, surprise group winners Belgium lost 2–1 to the mighty West Germany in the final.

### Platini excels

Under the management of Bobby Robson, England narrowly missed out on qualification for the 1984 tournament, held in France. For the first time, the finals comprised a group stage followed by semi-finals and the final.

England captain Bobby Moore is just too late to prevent Dzajic scoring Yugoslavia's winning goal in the semi-final of the 1968 European Nations Cup.

Inspired by their brilliant captain, Michel Platini, France were worthy winners, beating Spain 2–0 in the final.

### Robson woe

Robson's England travelled to West Germany for the 1988 tournament on a wave of optimism after remaining unbeaten in qualifying. England boasted the talent of Peter Shilton, Bryan Robson and Gary Lineker, among others. But embarrassing defeats against Ireland, Holland and the USSR saw England finish bottom of our group. The Dutch, blessed with the class of Rijkaard, Gullit and Van Basten, were crowned champions as they overcame the USSR in the final.

### Danish surprise

Further embarrassment awaited Graham Taylor's England in Sweden four years later. Listless draws against Denmark and France were followed by defeat by the host nation with David Platt's goal providing little consolation in England hero Gary Lineker's farewell match.

Denmark were late entrants to the finals, called up as a replacement for war-torn Yugoslavia. The Danes overcame champions Holland in a memorable semi-final penalty shoot-out before completing a surprise victory over Germany in the final.

### So close

In 1996, football finally came home and the finals were expanded to 16 teams. The host nation made an indifferent start though, drawing with Switzerland before finally coming to life against Scotland, an Alan Shearer goal and a brilliant strike by Paul Gascoigne sealing a 2–0 win. Satisfaction turned to euphoria as England thrashed the much-vaunted Dutch 4–1 with Alan Shearer and Teddy Sheringham bagging two each.

After beating Spain on penalties, Terry Venables' men made the perfect start when Shearer headed home after just three minutes of the semi-final showdown with arch-rivals Germany. But the Germans responded manfully to square the game.

The stalemate continued into extra-time but England looked the team more likely with Darren Anderton and Gazza agonisingly close to burying the winner. And so to the cruel lottery of penalties.

With the scores level, Gareth Southgate saw his spot-kick saved before Andy Möller converted to send Germany through to the final. The Germans went on to lift the trophy, beating the Czech Republic through Oliver Bierhoff's 'Golden Goal'.

### False start

England made a flying start to the 2000 finals in Belgium and Holland. Paul Scholes and Steve McManaman propelled Kevin Keegan's team to a 2–0 lead over Portugal in their opening match, but we collapsed to a demoralising 3–2 defeat.

Hope was restored when Shearer's second-half header sealed England's first major tournament victory over Germany since 1966. A draw against Romania would then be enough for England to qualify for the quarter-finals. But England failed to perform as a unit and, with the score at 2–2, disaster struck. On 88 minutes, Phil Neville made an ill-judged challenge, Ganea stroked home the resulting penalty and our Euro dreams were snatched away once more.

World Champions France went on to add the European crown to their trophy collection.

Alan Shearer proved his worth for England time and again – does the pose look familiar?

## RAUL | SPAIN

"Raul is an artist, more of a rounded footballer than van Nistelrooy. He is quick, can dribble well and is very very clever in the box. Many people think he is a centre-forward but he drops very deep at times. He is always there and always seems to score. He smells the danger."

# DESPERATELY SEEKING SVEN

**Think it's an easy life being the England boss? A match or two every couple of months and regular holidays to recover? Think again. Sven clocks up thousands of air miles every season to keep an eye on players' form. We tried to keep up with the indefatigable Swede in the month between England's final two Euro 2004 qualifiers against Liechtenstein and Turkey...**

1. 10 SEP 2003: ENGLAND v LIECHTENSTEIN
   OLD TRAFFORD
2. 13 SEP 2003: CHELSEA v TOTTENHAM HOTSPUR
   STAMFORD BRIDGE
3. 16 SEP 2003: MANCHESTER UNITED v PANATHINAIKOS
   OLD TRAFFORD
4. 17 SEP 2003: ARSENAL v INTERNAZIONALE
   HIGHBURY
5. 21 SEP 2003: TOTTENHAM HOTSPUR v SOUTHAMPTON
   WHITE HART LANE
6. 22 SEP 2003: MANCHESTER UNITED v ARSENAL
   OLD TRAFFORD
7. 26 SEP 2003: ARSENAL v NEWCASTLE UNITED
   HIGHBURY
8. 27 SEP 2003: CHELSEA v ASTON VILLA
   STAMFORD BRIDGE
9. 28 SEP 2003: CHARLTON ATHLETIC v LIVERPOOL
   THE VALLEY
10. 30 SEP 2003: ANDERLECHT v BAYERN MUNICH
    CONSTANT VANDEN STOCK STADIUM, BRUSSELS, BELGIUM
11. 1 OCT 2003: STUTTGART v MANCHESTER UNITED
    GOTTLIEB-DAIMLER-STADION, STUTTGART, GERMANY
12. EARLY OCTOBER: MEET UP WITH ENGLAND TEAM
    LONDON
13. 11 OCT 2003 TURKEY v ENGLAND
    SÜKRÜ SARAÇOGLU STADIUM, ISTANBUL

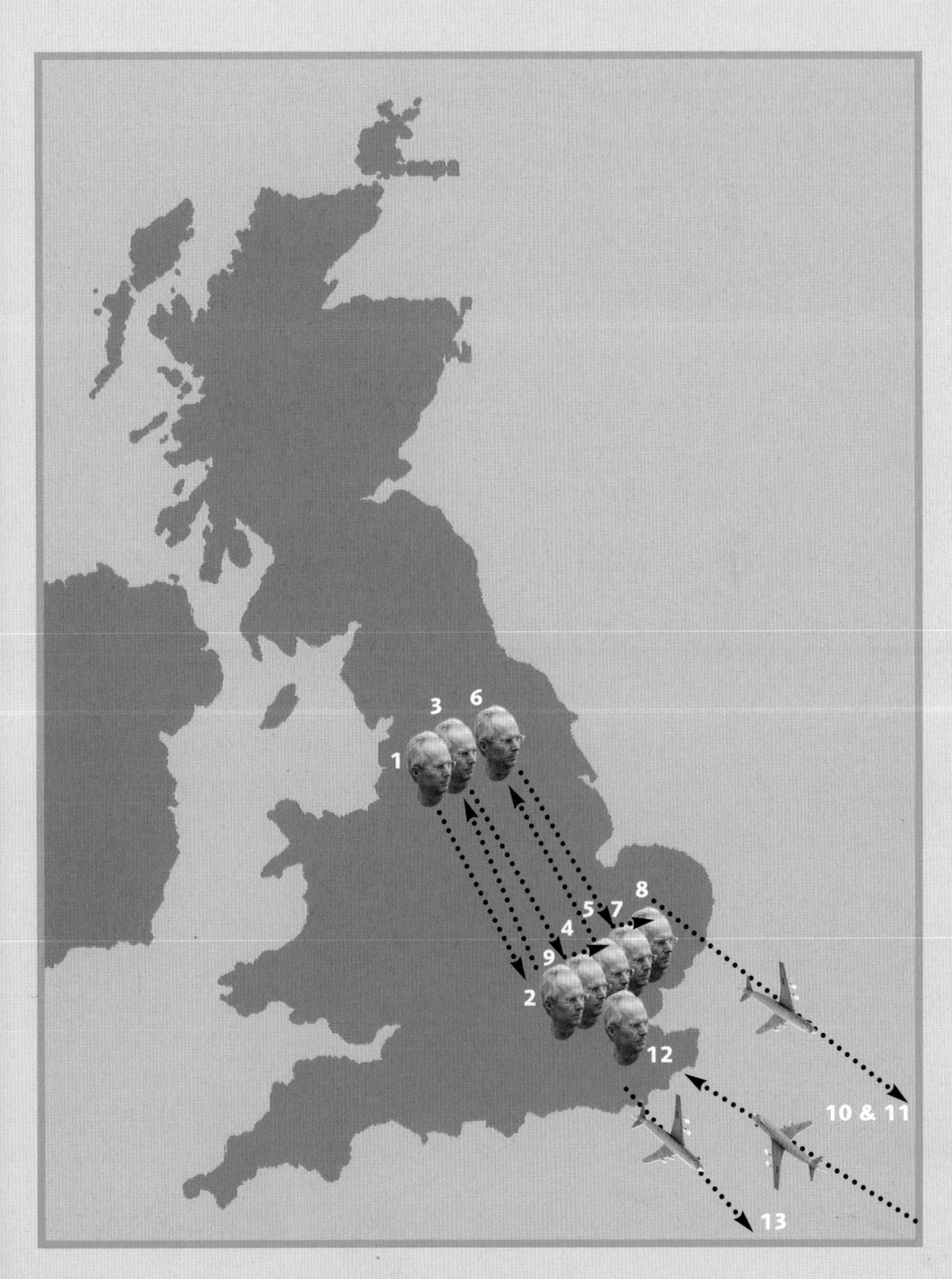


*To keep up-to-date with Sven's scouting missions, log on to the exclusive 'Sven tracker' at www.TheFA.com*

# SHOT STOPPER

**After years of trying in vain to shift 'Safe Hands' Seaman from the team, David James is determined to be England's number one in Portugal this summer...**

THERE WAS A TIME WHEN DAVID James would have considered virtually anything if he thought it could help him relieve David Seaman of the England number one shirt.

"I tried fishing, but I was no good at it," he smiles. "And I even toyed with the idea of a ponytail, but I bottled out. Long hair doesn't suit me!"

As he sits cradling a cup of tea in the canteen at Manchester City's training ground, James can afford to chuckle at his efforts to imitate Seaman. It has been a long time coming, but finally, seven years after Glenn Hoddle handed him an England debut in a friendly against Mexico (2–0, Sheringham and Fowler providing the goals, James the clean sheet), the 33-year-old has achieved his dream of becoming England's first-choice goalkeeper.

"Give David Seaman credit for the years he was the number one because he was the top performer," says James. "The competitors for the position just didn't maintain the same level that he did. David was outstanding and the rest of us weren't good enough."

Times have changed. At his age, relatively young for an international goalkeeper, James can at last look forward to a major championship confident that he will actually get to play. Over the last 18 months, Sven-Goran Eriksson's faith in the man has grown to such a degree that, barring injury, it seems almost inconceivable that anyone will wrest the jersey from his imposing six foot five inch frame.

What a difference a year makes. As his West Ham side slid to the bottom of the Premiership table last season, leaking goals left, right and centre, David feared that his England dream was in jeopardy just as Seaman's distinguished career was finally drawing to a close.

"You can't help but feel downhearted when the club's in that position and you're conceding goals," he admits, "but you just have to play the games and see what happens from there."

Despite his club's perilous position, James was selected in goal for the February 2003 friendly with Australia as part of Eriksson's first-choice team. A month later, he was back between the posts for the crucial Euro 2004 qualifiers away to Liechtenstein and against Turkey at the Stadium of Light. Two clean sheets, two victories: David has never looked back.

**"I've staked my claim for the shirt and I'd be very disappointed to lose it now"**

"My view on the England situation is that Eriksson picks on merit so it's up to me to maintain my form," he says. "I've staked my claim for the shirt and I'd be very disappointed to lose it now. If I can perform to my best, I hope to stay in the team."

West Ham's relegation to Division One at the end of last season might have harmed James' chances, but it did nothing to shake Eriksson's belief in his new first-choice keeper. David probably put it best himself: "As a goalkeeper, you have to just not let any goals in – no matter who kicks them."

He does concede, however, that at international level his powers of concentration are tested to the full.

"As a goalkeeper there are long periods of inactivity then, all of a sudden, the opposition get the ball and within 10 seconds they're down in your half. You have to be able to deal with that. I've done a lot of imagery work with a sports psychologist and I've got myself to the position where I'm prepared for that."

David knows his past will not simply go away – in Istanbul, where England's wonderful display clinched their place at Euro 2004, Turkey fans greeted him with 'Calamity' banners – but these days he lets criticism wash over him.

"The 'Calamity James' thing is a part of my history and I can't change that, but nowadays I don't care. I used to worry what people thought, but I don't waste mental energy on that any more. I used to read that I'd made 'great' saves when they were really nothing and 'howlers' when things weren't my fault so now I don't worry. I know whether or not I've played well."

And so does his manager.

"I'm a big fan of Eriksson," says David, finishing his tea. "He demonstrates authority. Me, I'm an authoritarian. I'd have joined the army if I hadn't gone into football. My brother did. Seriously, I like rules and people telling you what to do."

This summer, England fans have just one order for David James: win the trophy.

# LET'S PARTY!

**Not going to Portugal for the finals? Don't worry, our opposition-themed party tips, complete with 'who'll eat all the pies' recipes, could be the answer. Then again, it might not help at all...**

## ENGLAND v FRANCE

13 JUNE, 7.45PM

### MUSIC

In recent years there's been some decent French pop (no, not St Etienne) from the likes of Air and Phoenix but, if you want to appear achingly hip and a little worldly-wise, may we suggest a bit of Serge Gainsbourg on the stereo. The filthy ol' crooner was a bit of a ladies man and wrote some rather nice tunes. For the old folk, you could turn to another French crooner, albeit not so hip, Charles Asnavour. "Thank heavens for little girls" he once warbled in more innocent times. Which leads us to our last selection, professional pouter Vanessa Paradis (pictured above). Avoid the sticky early 'Joe Le Taxi' stuff and pick up a copy of the surprisingly not bad album she made with Lenny Kravitz.

### FOOD

The French pride themselves on their culinary skills and there is plenty to choose from if you search for "French cuisine" on the Internet: tartiflette or quiche are simple classics.

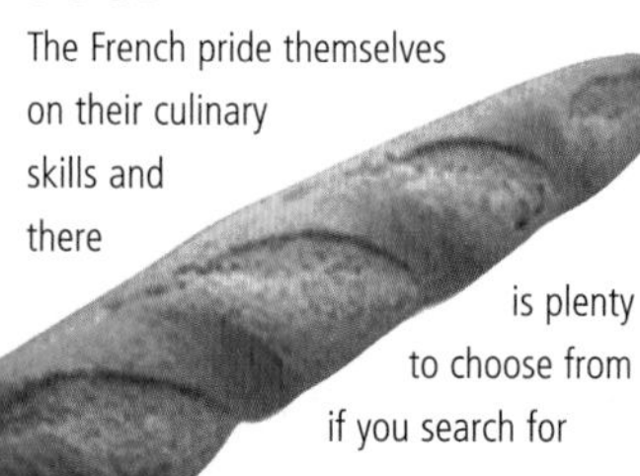

A more painless route to take might involve more simple fare – baguettes, paté and cheese will all keep your themed party on the right track and they're all enjoyable enough to consume as you watch Sven's lads storm into a three-goal lead in the first 10 minutes of the match (okay, that last bit might not be guaranteed).

### DRINK

The French have long been famous for their alcohol. You've got a multitude of great wines to choose from, and champagnes, beers and cognacs too. And, hey, there's always Orangina or Gini for the kids.

Our recommendations for sipping as you watch the match are Chateau Margaux (if you've got a hundred odd quid to spare) or, if like us your budget is closer to a fiver, remember that the French adore Le Piat d'Or – well that's what it says in the adverts.

### CLOTHING

French fashion has ruled the world at various times over the last century or so and some of the finest haute couture and Parisian chic emanates from across the Channel. So what Chanel outfit would we recommend you and your guests dress up in – a little black dress, a crisply tailored suit? Non, non, non... that's far too formal – it is a party after all. The French dress "European" these days, so casual chic is perfectly acceptable. After all, how many Frenchmen would accept a dress code?

### AND ANOTHER THING...

If you want to theme the whole day or afternoon leading up to the match you could do worse than have a French cinema marathon. Either with films set in France, such as the recent-ish 'Moulin Rouge' and its bizarre musical cross-pollinations (Elton John and Nirvana... eh?!) or with subtitles-and-everything proper French movie fare. In which case we'd recommend 'Betty Blue', with Beatrice Dalle, the stylish but very violent 'Le Haine' and the timeless 'Jules Et Jim'.

### 'WHO'LL EAT ALL THE PIES?' RECIPE

**French Meat Pie**

INGREDIENTS

3 pounds of braising steak
3 or 4 potatoes, diced
1 onion, chopped
1 cup water
1 egg white
salt & pepper
garlic
sage

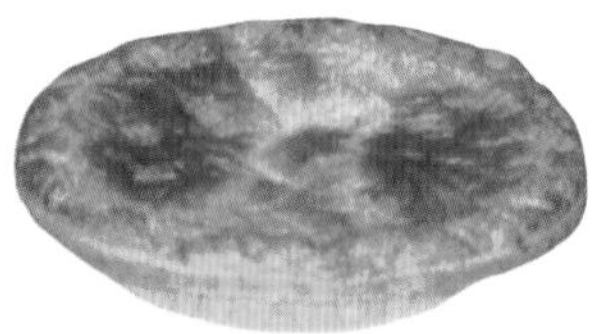

**Instructions**

Put all ingredients in a pan and bring to a boil. Add salt and pepper. Simmer for one to two hours.

Mash potatoes while they are cooking with the meat. Add one-and-a-half tablespoons of sage and two cloves of crushed garlic. Make pie crust and put in the pie pan.

Cover meat pie with top crust and bake at 350°F for 25 minutes or until crust is brown (brush the crust with one egg white and one tablespoon of water for a golden finish).

Serve when piping hot.

# ENGLAND v SWITZERLAND

17 JUNE, 5PM

## MUSIC

Apart from that strange duo Yello (remember 'The Race'?) we were a little stumped trying to work out other Swiss popsters to get your party started. Our guess is you don't own albums by Popmonster ("Radiohead meets the Beatles" apparently, with a female singer) or Kartagon ("Dark electro meets future pop"). And then it came to us – yodelling! To get in the mood, have a listen to Robert Palmer's 'Change His Ways', one of the few songs to bring yodelling into the mainstream!

## FOOD

Everybody knows the Swiss make very nice chocolate so plenty of that will probably go down well. But if you're looking for something a little more savoury then try a bit of cheesy fondue (careful, it can get messy). Other cheesy dishes popular in Switzerland include 'raclette'. A large half-round of special raclette cheese is held in front of a fire, and as it melts it's scraped (raclé) onto a plate, and served with boiled potatoes, pearl onions and pickles.

And for desert, er, Swiss rolls, anyone?

## DRINK

Um, we know this is chocolate again, but the Swiss do enjoy hot chocolate in a bowl. However, some of your fellow revellers may be chocced out by now, so perhaps a stein of beer at this point would be a good idea. Coffee is also very popular. As well as normal espresso, cappuccino and the rest, local variations include 'Kaffee crème' (coffee with sugar and cream), 'Milchkaffee', (coffee with fresh milk) and 'Kaffee fertig' (coffee with Schnapps!)

## CLOTHING

You can go two ways: either to the slopes or to the sauna. If you go the slopes route then it's just a case of everyone turning up in big ski jackets, salopettes, snow shoes, the works. Just wearing ski goggles and snowshoes (or better still, skis!) in the front room will make everyone look suitably ridiculous.

The sauna option is even easier – it's towels all round!

## AND ANOTHER THING...

Switzerland isn't a country famous for its movies, but here are a couple that were made there: Seventies' French beard-fest "Claire's Knee" and the rather odd love story "Yvonne's Perfume".

## RECIPE

**'Pastetli' Pie**

1 pound of puff-pastry; 2 tablespoons of butter; 1 shallot, hacked; 1 clove of garlic, pressed, 1.75 pounds of small mushrooms, each cut into four pieces; 3.4 fluid ounces of white wine; 1 small tub of soured cream; 1 tablespoon Worcestershire sauce; 1 teaspoon each – paprika, nutmeg, cayenne pepper and salt.

**Instructions**

Bake six large heart-shaped pies made out of the puff-pastry for about 15 to 20 minutes. Heat margarine or butter in a pot. Add shallot and clove of garlic, stew. Add white wine and mushrooms, mix, cover and cook for about five minutes. Increase heat, cook in open pot until half of the fluid has gone. Add soured cream, Worcestershire sauce, all the spices and salt. Distribute the filling into the heated pies. Serve immediately.

# ENGLAND v CROATIA

21 JUNE, 7.45PM

## MUSIC

You'll have to take our word for it, but it's true: the Teletubbies have actually inspired an album by a Croatian jazz ensemble! We haven't heard it but suspect it's a noo-noo (do you see what we did there?).

## FOOD

Croatians love their seafood such as sardines and anchovies. Other staples include smoked and dried meats such as 'csabai' (lots of paprika and garlic) and cabbage rolls (both fresh and canned). Other specialities include salmon preserved in lime, poppy seed cakes, walnut cakes and Croatian digestive teas.

## DRINK

In Croatia they like their ale and, probably the best of the native brews is Karlovacko Karlovacko. Our beer connoisseur mate describes it as having "a smooth and distinct flavour and it doesn't give you a headache the next day." Hoorah!

## CLOTHING

In the 17th century, Croatian soldiers within the Napoleon army were spotted wearing particular scarves around their necks as part of their standard uniforms. This "Croatian Style" became very popular among French noblemen in the 17th century and soon the fashionable expression in French "a la croate" became the word which, in many languages, still resembles the name of Croatia – the homeland of the Cravate. So get all your guests to wear ties!

## AND ANOTHER THING...

Dalmatian dogs originate from Dalmatia in Croatia (well, it was actually a section of Yugoslavia back then), so you could all sit down and watch the '101 Dalmatians' film (cartoon version) before the game. Or perhaps you might get everyone to dress up as Cruella De Ville... or maybe not!

## RECIPE

**'Burek' Meat Pie**

Although of Turkish origin, this is very popular in Croatia as a light meal.

INGREDIENTS

Filo (or puff) pastry
5.5oz lean beef
5.5oz onion
salt & pepper
1.5oz vegetable oil

**Instructions**

Fry the finely chopped onions and minced meat in oil. Add the salt and pepper. Grease a round baking tray and put a layer of pastry in it.Cover with a thin layer of filling and cover this with another filo pastry layer which must be well coated in oil. Put another layer of filling and cover with pastry. When you have five or six layers, cover with filo pastry, bake at 390°F for half an hour and cut into quarters and serve.

# HOMECOMING - ENGLAND'S RETURN TO WEMBLEY STADIUM

**In early 2006, the England Team will return to their spiritual home: Wembley Stadium, the Venue of Legends. With work ahead of schedule, the new stadium is fast taking shape and it's likely Wembley will be opened with a prestigious England international before the 2006 FIFA World Cup Finals.**

THE NEW WEMBLEY WILL BE THE BIGGEST AND BEST STADIUM IN THE WORLD. Seating 90,000 fans, everyone will enjoy unobstructed views of the action and state-of-the-art facilities. Three times the size of the Millennium Stadium in Cardiff, Wembley will use 23,000 tonnes of steel and 90,000 cubic metres of concrete and the roof will cover an incredible eleven acres! It will also boast some unique features that will set it apart from other stadiums:

**'AVE IT AT WEMBLEY!**
**In a survey by Club Wembley, fans voted Bolton comedian Peter Kay as the celebrity they'd most like to sit next to at a football match at Wembley.**

- **The pitch – thanks to a retractable roof, the pitch will be bathed in sunshine, allowing a lush natural pitch to grow, while protecting the fans from the elements.**
- **The atmosphere – acoustic engineering has ensured that the atmosphere at the new stadium will be even better than the old – the 'Wembley Roar' will be louder than ever.**
- **The arch – replacing the twin towers as the face of Wembley Stadium is a 133-metre high arch that holds up the roof and will be visible to fans from miles around as they come to the game.**

With 90,000 fans close to the pitch, Wembley will be an intimidating arena for visiting teams and should give the Three Lions an important edge over the opposition and create some unforgettable nights for the fans.

When it opens, Wembley will host all of The FA's major events, including The FA Cup Final and England internationals, plus a host of other major sports and music events. This line-up, combined with the unbeatable atmosphere and facilities that the new stadium will offer, makes Wembley a mouth-watering prospect for fans. Already, supporters who want to guarantee their place at the big games for ten years have reserved thousands of Club Wembley seats.

## RUUD VAN NISTELROOY | HOLLAND

"A classic centre-forward who has everything. He is strong, can keep the ball, he's quick – he is for me the complete centre-forward.

"The thing with Van Nistelrooy is that he can score goals with both his feet as well as his head and this makes him very dangerous – you can never relax!

"I think he will play for Holland at Euro 2004 – how could you leave him out?"

# HITMAN

**Michael Owen possesses a deadly combination of speed and cold-blooded finishing skills. Europe, be very afraid...**

GOALS. THAT'S REALLY ALL THERE IS to it. When you think of Michael Owen, you think of goals: vital strikes at the highest level; magnificent efforts in the biggest matches; yes, even run-of-the-mill tap-ins from a few yards. They all count and Owen happily takes them all.

The former European Footballer of the Year strikes fear into the heart of every goalkeeper in Europe.

The qualifiers for this year's European Championship were a case in point.

England started the campaign in Bratislava where, with eight minutes to go we appeared to be heading for a 1–1 draw with Slovakia. Until Owen popped up to nudge home the winner.

He followed up with the breakthrough goal against Liechtenstein, a header this time. Then he struck twice to beat Slovakia at home and once again to send Liechtenstein to another defeat. Five goals was a tidy return but hardly a surprise to his manager. Ask Sven about his striker and the England manager will wax lyrical.

"For me, Michael is something very special. His technique is excellent but he has two things which are difficult to find in a football player: He's very cold when he gets an opportunity and he's very, very quick. When you have that combination of skills it's a killer."

As a shell-shocked Oliver Kahn admitted after the German goalkeeper had conceded five (yes, it was five, wasn't it?!) in *that* match against England:

"We just could not stop Michael Owen over the 90 minutes. We were always struggling to keep up with him. He was so cold and clinical."

So what goes through the mind of a cold-blooded killer striker when he scores a goal? Obviously, there are plenty you could get him to talk through but, what the hell, let's choose arguably his most spectacular to date: that famous World Cup strike against Argentina at France '98

"I think I'll have seen this a million times before I die," says Michael with a slight touch of relish. Roll VT!

It's 16 minutes into the game, the scores are level at 1–1. David Beckham chips a beautiful ball to Michael who controls it without breaking his stride, picks up his pace and starts running towards the first defender, Chamot.

**"We must believe we can do well in Portugal. That's the important thing. But if I can score some goals that help us do that, I'll be happy."**

"At this point, I'm just sizing up my options," says Michael. "I thought he was going to bring me down. But I got past him, kept running, started to build up pace. Then I looked up and saw the sweeper, Roberto Ayala, in my way. But I'm still not thinking about going for goal. I just wanted to get past him."

Owen veers to the right to get past as Paul Scholes moves in, possibly to take possession.

"I wasn't even aware of Paul coming in. Once I was past the sweeper, it all opened up and my only thought was hitting it past the keeper. As it went past him, I suppose I must have thought, 'This could be a bit memorable if it goes in.'"

So how does it feel to score an exceptional goal like that?

"At moments like that," he grins, "it's difficult to remain calm and collected. It's hard to keep your emotions down. The energy is pumping so much. At that moment, it's like your mind doesn't actually belong to you. Of course, every goal is special in its own way. But, when you score one like that, it's a bit more special. It's the kind of goal you dream of scoring when you're a kid, just kicking the ball around in the playground. Then it happens like that. Unbelievable. To play in games like that. To score goals like that. It's what it's all about."

And does he think he might score another like it in Portugal this summer?

"Well, I've no interest in scoring a great goal and England getting beaten. But I could handle another game like the Germany match. That was a much better experience, one of the best moments of my career so far. You can dream about scoring a hat-trick but you don't think it is going to come true. It was unbelievable. Everyone prays for those moments. I'm fortunate that it has happened to me but it only did because everyone in the team played their part. And as a team, we're still getting better. We must believe we can do well in Portugal. That's the important thing. But if I can score some goals that help us do that, I'll be happy."

Spoken like a cold-blooded striker. France, Croatia, Switzerland and co, watch out...

Italy

Greece

England

Switzerland

Spain

Croatia

Portugal

Denmark

Russia

Latvia

Germany

Bulgaria

France

# THE CONTENDERS

The top 16 international teams in Europe will be competing to win the famous Henri Delaunay trophy this summer. Check out our team-by-team guide to the big guns, dark horses and surprise qualifiers…

Sweden

Czech Republic

Holland

# PORTUGAL

**With a World Cup winner in charge and some exciting young talent coming through, the host nation have high hopes...**

**For Rui Costa, seen here shadowed by England's Nicky Butt, Euro 2004 is the last-chance saloon.**

If you can't beat them, appoint them. That was Portugal's idea when, after years of under-achievement, they gave Brazil's World Cup-winning coach Luiz Felipe Scolari the task of leading them into Euro 2004.

A succession of native coaches had failed to get the best out of Portugal's fabled "golden generation" in the years since they won the World Youth Championships in 1989 and 1991, so for the first time in over three decades they turned to a foreign coach. Two years ago, Scolari took a disparate Brazilian squad and transformed them into world champions in the space of a year. Now the Portuguese are hoping he can repeat the trick for them.

So far the Brazilian's progress has been patchy. The high point was their 2–1 victory over his old charges, Brazil, last year, but there has also been a 0–3 defeat to Spain, who they will meet again in the group stage at Euro 2004, a 1–0 defeat to Italy, and an unconvincing 1–0 win over Kazakhstan.

The main problem for the Portuguese is that they have been stuck in a 'Groundhog Day' of friendlies. After two years without a competitive game, Scolari is well aware his players must adopt what he calls "a different attitude" this summer.

Scolari has worked hard to reduce the average age of his team, dispensing with several players including such legends as 33-year-old Vitor Baia and 31-year-old Joao Pinto

"To change things I had to change names," says Scolari.

What is left is a squad of some "golden generation" veterans and a new crop of exciting young players.

Luis Figo, Rui Costa and Fernando Couto are now all in their early thirties, so Euro 2004 represents their last chance to win a major tournament. Spurred on by home crowds, they are capable of going all the way. However, there is also a real fear that collectively they might have already seen their best days.

Fortunately, a new group of players has emerged just in time. Manchester United's Cristiano Ronaldo, Barcelona's Ricardo Quaresma and Benfica's Tiago Mendes will inject some unpredictability, but this tournament might have come too early for them. Indeed, apart from Porto playmaker Deco, Portugal have few players at their absolute peak.

Can Scolari find the right blend of these two generations of players? It's a hard task, but he is relishing the challenge. "We have 24 days to shine in June," he says. "I'm confident we will produce something of beauty."

**MANAGER**
**LUIZ FELIPE SCOLARI**

After an unexceptional playing career, Scolari began coaching in the early eighties. He has since won the South American championship, and the Copa Libertadores on two occasions (with Gremio in 1995 and Palmeiras in 1999). An unpopular appointment as Brazil's coach in June 2001, he went on to win the country's fifth World Cup a year later.

**ONE TO WATCH**
**CRISTIANO RONALDO**

Ronaldo had only played 29 professional games when Manchester United paid Sporting Lisbon £12.24 million for him last summer. Since then the 18-year-old winger has proved to be a rare and exciting talent in the Premiership, and has made his international debut for Portugal. "I can see similarities between him and Figo," says Scolari.

## PORTUGAL ESSENTIALS

◎ Portugal's last competitive game against Spain was a group match at the 1984 European Championship, which ended in a 1–1 draw.

◎ Portugal played their first international match in 1921, losing 3–1 to Spain in Madrid.

### THE ROAD TO EURO 2004

Portugal qualified automatically as tournament hosts.

**GROUP A FIXTURES**

12 June v Greece, Porto 5pm*
16 June v Russia, Lisbon, 7.45pm
20 June v Spain, Lisbon, 7.45pm

**All match kick-off times listed are BST.*

# GREECE

**They've never won a game at a European Championship finals, but can this well-drilled Greece team finally break their duck in Portugal?**

**Any team will do well to score against this lot...**

It would be fair to say the Greeks don't have the best record at major championships. Before they made it to Euro 2004, they had only ever qualified for two tournaments, where they failed to win a game and managed just one goal in a combined 540 minutes.

Greece went out in the first round of the 1980 European Championship after defeats to Czechoslovakia and Holland, and a draw with West Germany. Fourteen years later at the World Cup in the USA they suffered a bit and went home early again after losing all three games of their games by an aggregate of 10–0.

The German coach Otto Rehhagel was asked to re-energise Greek football, but even he was shocked at the quality of his new charges when he took over.

"I have rarely seen players play like that," he said at the time. "They were without desire and losing almost every challenge throughout the match."

Will the Greek class of 2004 be any different? Initially, it appeared not in the qualifiers. They meekly lost their opening two games to Spain and the Ukraine without scoring a goal. But then they discovered some resilience and went on a run of six consecutive wins to finish top of their group and claim a place in this summer's finals tournament.

The secret to this sharp turnaround was Rehhagel instilling a German mentality into his players, with the result being they didn't concede a single goal in that run of six wins, and of the 16 teams at Euro 2004 only France and Sweden can boast a better defensive record in the qualifiers.

The one result that flooded the Greeks with confidence was their 1–0 win over Spain in Zaragoza in June 2003 courtesy of a winner from Bolton's Stelios Giannakopoulos. A hard-fought draw with Euro 2004 hosts Portugal in a friendly last November has also given them reason to believe they can prosper this summer.

The Greeks will be difficult to score against; their back four of Giourkas Seitaridis, Stylianos Venetidis, Nikos Dabizas and Traianos Dellas has not conceded a competitive goal since October 2002, and Rehhagel has even been known to use a sweeper for added protection. However, at the other end the Greeks are surprisingly impotent in attack and only scored 8 goals in qualifying, the lowest total of all the 16 teams at Euro 2004.

"We don't want to go to Portugal just to represent Greece, we want to achieve something there... So far I have had a lot of fun in this job," says Rehhagel. The fun could be about to stop; the Greeks appear too imbalanced and inexperienced to get beyond the group stages, and they might be forced to wait even longer for that first-ever win at a major championship.

**MANAGER**
**OTTO REHHAGEL**

The 64-year-old coach spent his entire career in Germany before taking the Greece job in 2001. As a player, he was a centre-half for Berlin and Kaiserslautern, and as a coach, he enjoyed his greatest successes with Werder Bremen, leading them to two Bundesliga titles, two German Cups and a Cup-Winners' Cup.

**ONE TO WATCH**
**DIMITRIS PAPADOPOULOS**

The 22-year-old Panathinaikos striker played no part in the qualifying campaign, but with their lack of goals, he is expected to force his way in to the squad for Euro 2004. A regular in the Under-21s and a leading scorer in the Greek League, Papadopoulos has only made two first-team appearances.

## GREECE ESSENTIALS

◎ Only five players scored for Greece in qualifying for Euro 2004: Vassilios Tsiartas, Angelos Charisteas, Stelios Giannakopoulos, Themistoklis Nikolaidis and Zisis Vryzas.

◎ By the end of 2003, Greece had remained unbeaten in 11 consecutive friendlies.

### THE ROAD TO EURO 2004

**UEFA QUALIFYING GROUP 6**

07/09/02 v Spain (h) lost 0–2
12/10/02 v Ukraine (a) lost 0–2
16/10/02 v Armenia (h) won 2–0
02/04/03 v N Ireland (a) won 2–0
07/06/03 v Spain (a) won 1–0
11/06/03 v Ukraine (h) won 1–0
06/09/03 v Armenia (a) won 1–0
11/10/03 v N Ireland (h) won 1–0

**TOP SCORER**

Angelos Charisteas, 3 goals

**FINAL POSITION**

| P | W | D | L | F | A | GD | Pts | Psn |
|---|---|---|---|---|---|---|---|---|
| 8 | 6 | 0 | 2 | 8 | 4 | +4 | 18 | 1st |

**GROUP A FIXTURES**

12 June v Portugal, Porto, 5pm
16 June v Spain, Porto, 5pm
20 June v Russia, Faro-Loulé, 7.45pm

# SPAIN

**A team bursting with talent and flair, Spain have the credentials to go all the way and win the trophy... Hmm, how many times have we heard that before?**

**MANAGER**
**INAKI SAEZ**
The 60-year-old was promoted from within when Camacho resigned in 2002. As director of Spain's youth teams, he won an impressive haul including a silver medal at the 2000 Olympic Games and gold in the 2002 Under-19 Championship.

**ONE TO WATCH**
**FERNANDO TORRES**
Since debuting for Atletico Madrid aged 16, Torres has established himself as one of the most promising strikers in Europe. Keen to prove he can partner Raul for the national team, he was La Liga's second highest scorer at Christmas.

## SPAIN ESSENTIALS

◎ The Spanish coach Inaki Saez was forced to miss his son's wedding to be in charge of Spain's first play-off game against Norway in November last year.

◎ In the last five European Championships that they have qualified for, Spain have twice gone out in the first round, in 1980 and 1988.

### THE ROAD TO EURO 2004

**UEFA QUALIFYING GROUP 6**
07/09/02 v Greece (a) won 2–0
12/10/02 v N Ireland (h) won 3–0
29/03/03 v Ukraine (a) drew 2–2
02/04/03 v Armenia (h) won 3–0
07/06/03 v Greece (h) lost 0–1
11/06/03 v N Ireland (a) drew 0–0
10/09/03 v Ukraine (h) won 2–1
11/10/03 v Armenia (a) won 4–0

**FINAL POSITION**

| P | W | D | L | F | A | GD | Pts | Psn |
|---|---|---|---|---|---|---|---|---|
| 8 | 5 | 2 | 1 | 16 | 4 | +12 | 17 | 2nd |

**PLAY-OFFS**
15/11/03 v Norway (h) won 2–1
19/11/03 v Norway (a) won 3–0

**TOP SCORER**
Raul, 7 goals

**GROUP A FIXTURES**
12 June v Russia, Faro-Loulé, 7.45pm
16 June v Greece, Porto, 5pm
20 June v Portugal, Lisbon, 7.45pm

While the Spanish can boast of a thriving domestic league, a national squad overflowing with talent and a FIFA ranking that says they are the third best team in the world behind Brazil and France, they still have not managed to win a major championship since 1964. Can the serial under-achievers end their own 40 years of hurt?

Spain's start to their qualifying campaign suggested they could; they topped their group and remained unbeaten after four games, drawing with the Ukraine and beating Greece, Northern Ireland and Armenia without conceding a goal.

But the old doubts began to surface when Spain suffered the shock of losing 1–0 to Greece on home soil in June last year. "That provoked some really bad moments for us," says Raul.

This showed in the following game when they could only secure a goalless draw with Northern Ireland.

Inaki Saez steadied his team and they won their two remaining qualifying games, but this wasn't good enough to dislodge Greece from the top of the group and they had to settle for a play-off place. The Spanish showed their true class by overcoming the Norwegians 5–1 over two games, most impressively winning 3–0 in Oslo.

"We have always qualified brilliantly in the past and ended up not winning anything, so maybe this time we can bring home the success that Spanish football needs," says Raul.

But even getting out of a group also featuring Portugal, Greece and Russia might be difficult. The Greeks have already proved they can beat them and the Portuguese will be tough opponents in their own backyard.

But if, and it is always a big if with the Spanish, they perform to their potential they could go far this summer. In between the posts, Spain have the young but experienced Iker Casillas (Santiago Canizares provides back-up), while in defence are his Real Madrid team-mates Ivan Helguera, Michel Salgado and Raul Bravo, who are assisted by Barcelona's fearsome Carlos Puyol. Only four goals got past this defence in the qualifiers.

**Even the talented Deportivo playmaker Juan Valeron isn't guaranteed a place in Spain's midfield.**

Spain's midfield is monopolised by Valencia; Ruben Baraja and David Albelda in the centre and Vicente Rodriguez on the right provide flair and work-rate. They can be complimented by either Athletico Bilbao's Joseba Etxeberría or Real Betis' Joaquín Sánchez on the left, and a choice of gifted playmaker Xabi Alonso or Juan Valeron through the middle.

For all this talent, so much still rests on the form of Raul. It is crucial for Spain's chances that their leading all-time goal scorer (38 goals in 69 games) repeats what he does so often in a Real Madrid shirt. A conveyor belt of young talent including Jose Antonio Reyes, Fernando Torres, Diego Tristan, Albert Luque, and Miguel Mista is battling for the honour of partnering Raul up front.

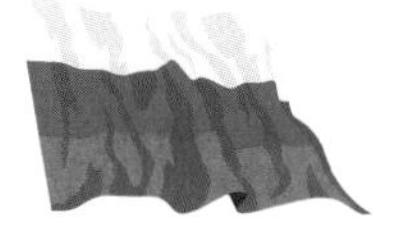

# RUSSIA

**Halfway through the qualifying campaign the president of Russian football said God couldn't save them, but a simple change of coach resurrected their fortunes**

If Russia were hosting this summer's European Championship, they would have to start as one of the favourites. Just look at their qualifying record; at home they were utterly ruthless, winning their four games 4–2, 4–1, 4–1 and 3–1. But as soon as they ventured outside their borders, they became a completely different team and failed to win a single one of their away qualifiers.

**Experienced players such as Celta Vigo captain Alexander Mostovoi were brought back into the fold to clinch Russia's place at Euro 2004.**

The Russians started on the road to Portugal with two comprehensive home wins against Ireland and Albania, but then suffered consecutive defeats on their trips to Albania and Georgia, while only managing to draw in Switzerland. It was this inconsistency, coupled with an embarrassing friendly defeat to Israel, which forced Valeri Gazzayev to resign as Russian coach in August last year.

At the same time Vyacheslav Koloskov, the president of the Russian football federation, launched a stinging attack on his squad.

"Even if God himself was our coach he would not have saved us," he said. "I told the players straight to their faces they should be ashamed of themselves but apparently they weren't.They must realise the responsibility for such a shambles is with them."

The former Spartak Moscow coach Georgi Yartsev became his country's sixth coach in the last 11 years when he was given a six-week contract and three games to salvage Russia's Euro 2004 qualifying campaign. Yartsev's first act was to bring back a raft of experienced players Gazzayev had discarded, including Celta Vigo's captain Alexander Mostovoi, Porto's Dmitri Alenichev and the clubless Viktor Onopko. "They have not yet exhausted their potential," said Yartsev.

Yartsev's words were soon vindicated as Russia claimed a point against the Republic of Ireland in Dublin before thrashing Switzerland and Georgia back at home to set up a play-off against Wales. The Russians were disciplined in their two games against the Welsh, drawing 0–0 in Moscow before finally winning away, 1–0 in Cardiff.

Yartsev has certainly injected some confidence into the Russian ranks, but that alone won't be enough to genuinely compete in Portugal. While they have plenty of experience, their defence, which conceded more goals in the qualifiers than any of the other teams at Euro 2004 and their poor away form – could mean that the team have their work cut out if they are going to qualify for the knockout stages.

**MANAGER**
**GEORGI YARTSEV**

The former Soviet international had been unemployed for three years when he was handed the job of rescuing Russia's Euro 2004 qualifying campaign in August last year. He had earlier built his reputation as a coach at Spartak and Dynamo Moscow and Rotor Volgograd.

**ONE TO WATCH**
**DMITRI BULYKIN**

The 23-year-old Dynamo Moscow striker has looked a natural on the international stage since being given his debut against Ireland in September 2003. He didn't score that day, but managed four goals in his first three appearances, including a hat-trick against Switzerland.

## RUSSIA ESSENTIALS

- This is the first time Russia has qualified since the break-up of the former Soviet Union in 1991.
- As the Soviet Union, Russia won the competition in 1960.

### THE ROAD TO EURO 2004

**UEFA QUALIFYING GROUP 10**

07/09/02 v Rep of Ireland (h) won 4–2
16/10/02 v Albania (h) won 4–1
29/03/03 v Albania (a) lost 1–3
30/04/03 v Georgia (a) lost 0–1
07/06/03 v Switzerland (a) drew 2–2
06/09/03 v Rep of Ireland (a) drew 1–1
10/09/03 v Switzerland (h) won 4–1
11/10/03 v Georgia (h) won 3–1

**TOP SCORERS**

Sergei Ignashevitch and Dmitri Bulykin, 3 goals

**FINAL POSITION**

| P | W | D | L | F | A | GD | Pts | Psn |
|---|---|---|---|---|---|---|---|---|
| 8 | 4 | 2 | 2 | 19 | 12 | +7 | 14 | 2nd |

**PLAY-OFFS**

15/11/03 v Wales (h) drew 0–0
19/11/03 v Wales (a) won 1–0

**GROUP A FIXTURES**

12 June v Spain, Faro-Loulé, 7.45pm
16 June v Portugal, Lisbon, 7.45pm
20 June v Greece, Faro Loulé, 7.45pm

# FRANCE

**Pires, Vieira, Zidane, Henry... defending champs France clearly have the talent but can they recapture the magic of Euro 2000?**

**MANAGER**
**JACQUES SANTINI**
A battling midfielder in the renowned St Etienne side of the Seventies, Santini went on to coach Toulouse, Lille and FCSM. His greatest achievement was winning Le Championnat with Lyon before he replaced Roger Lemerre after the 2002 World Cup.

**ONE TO WATCH**
**DAVID TREZEGUET**
The 26 year-old Juventus striker was the French hero at the last European Championship when he scored the golden-goal winner against Italy in the final. Since then he has enjoyed a constant stream of goals and silverware in Serie A, as well as amassing an impressive international record of 19 goals in 43 appearances.

## FRANCE ESSENTIALS

◎ The French captain Marcel Desailly won his 100th international cap in their 5–0 win over Slovenia in the Euro 2004 qualifiers.

◎ France have won the European Championship twice, in 1984 and 2000.

### THE ROAD TO EURO 2004

**UEFA QUALIFYING GROUP 1**
07/09/02 v Cyprus (a) won 2–1
12/10/02 v Slovenia (h) won 5–0
16/10/02 v Malta (a) won 4–0
29/03/03 v Malta (h) won 6–0
02/04/03 v Israel (a) won 2–1
06/09/03 v Cyprus (h) won 5–0
10/09/03 v Slovenia (a) won 2–0
11/10/03 v Israel (h) won 3–0

**TOP SCORERS**
David Trezeguet, Thierry Henry and Sylvain Wiltord, 5 goals

**FINAL POSITION**

| P | W | D | L | F | A | GD | Pts | Psn |
|---|---|---|---|---|---|---|---|---|
| 8 | 8 | 0 | 0 | 29 | 2 | +27 | 24 | 1st |

**GROUP B FIXTURES**
13 June v England, Lisbon, 7.45pm
17 June v Croatia, Leiria, 7.45pm
21 June v Sw'land, Coimbra, 7.45pm

So it was a blip after all. France's humiliation at the last World Cup when they were knocked out in the first round seemed to suggest their golden era was over, but by scorching their way through qualifying for Euro 2004 they will now travel to Portugal as favourites to defend their title.

'Les Bleus' won all their qualifying games to become only the third team to achieve this in the tournament's history; they scored 29 goals, more than any other team in the Euro 2004 qualifiers, and conceded just two goals, the fewest of any other team. Throw in their busy schedule of friendlies and by last Christmas France had won a staggering 13 consecutive games to set a new national record.

Lessons had to be learned from the World Cup. As Lilian Thuram says, "We saw ourselves as too beautiful." There was also speculation of a split in the French camp between veterans and young players, but this has now been banished and replaced with a cohesive and focused squad.

This is a team almost bereft of any weaknesses: Fabien Barthez, out of favour with Manchester United, is still the French number one goalkeeper for the simple reason that he has never let the national team down. Protecting him is a back four of Thuram, Marcel Desailly, Mikael Silvestre and Bixente Lizarazu that drains even the best strikers of their confidence.

It doesn't seem fair that the French can call on both Claude Makelele and Patrick Vieira for the holding roles in midfield, while around them Robert Pires, Zinedine Zidane and Sylvain Wiltord are free to perform. At 31, Zidane remains the world's best player and is still capable of inspiring his team-mates to yet another triumph this summer.

Zidane's only competition for the title of the world's best player is provided by his team-mate, Thierry

Danger: genius at work.

Henry. The Arsenal striker has been bewitching defences around Europe for several seasons now and just seems to get better. If Henry is in the mood, it is difficult to see him being stopped.

The French will be happy with their first-round group; the England game will be tough, but they will expect Croatia and Switzerland to pose less of a problem. In just over a year at the helm of France, Jacques Santini has not lost a competitive game, and it is a record he could still have at the end of Euro 2004. Don't be surprised to see Desailly holding aloft the Henri Delaunay trophy on 4 July.

# ENGLAND

**Very hard to beat and boasting a healthy mix of youth and experience, this England team is in with a real chance...**

**MANAGER**
**SVEN-GORAN ERIKSSON**
Sven-Goran Eriksson's three-year reign as England coach has been one of almost undiluted success. He has qualified for both the 2002 World Cup and Euro 2004, losing only one competitive game along the way. No wonder The FA has already offered him a contract extension.

**ONE TO WATCH**
**JOE COLE**
Hailed as the "future of English football" before he had even made his professional debut, Joe Cole has finally been proving his talent with both England and Chelsea in the last year. The 22-year-old might not start at Euro 2004, but he will play an important role coming off the bench and adding his guile and creativity to midfield.

## ENGLAND ESSENTIALS

◎ England did not concede a single goal in the second half of our eight Euro 2004 qualifiers.

◎ England have never won the European Championship, but we have twice reached the semi-finals, in 1968 and 1996.

## THE ROAD TO EURO 2004

**UEFA QUALIFYING GROUP 7**
12/10/02 v Slovakia (a) won 2–1
16/10/02 v Macedonia (h) drew 2–2
29/03/03 v Liech'stein (a) won 2–0
02/04/03 v Turkey (h) won 2–0
11/06/03 v Slovakia (h) won 2–1
06/09/03 v Macedonia (a) won 2–1
10/09/03 v Liech'stein (h) won 2–0
11/10/03 v Turkey (a) drew 0–0

**TOP SCORERS:**
Michael Owen and David Beckham, 5 goals

**FINAL POSITION:**

| P | W | D | L | F | A | GD | Pts | Psn |
|---|---|---|---|---|---|---|---|---|
| 8 | 6 | 2 | 0 | 14 | 5 | +9 | 20 | 1st |

**GROUP B FIXTURES**
13 June v France, Lisbon, 7.45pm
17 June v Switz'land, Coimbra, 5pm
21 June v Croatia, Lisbon, 7.45pm

The scenes of England's victorious rugby players holding aloft the William Webb Ellis trophy in Sydney, slowly nosing their way through the streets of London on an open-top bus in front of 750,000 people and taking tea with the Queen will have made a huge impact on the England football team. They must know all of that glory could be theirs as well if they arrive home on 5 July as European champions.

"I can't say we will win Euro 2004, but we're good enough to win it," says Sven-Goran Eriksson. "We're one of a few teams that have that ability because in a real game it's not that easy to beat England any more."

He's right. England have only lost one of our last 19 competitive games, and last year set a national record with eight consecutive victories.

With the exception of that 2–1 defeat to Brazil in the World Cup quarter-finals, England have consistently proved they are a team for the big occasion over the last two and a half years. Just look at the evidence: Germany were convincingly beaten 5–1 on home turf in Munich, Argentina lost 1–0 at the World Cup, and Turkey were overcome in the Euro 2004 qualifiers as England won 2–0 at home and held out for a 0–0 draw in Istanbul.

The draw for Euro 2004 has been relatively kind to England. Obviously there are no easy games in a European Championship, but the draw could have been worse: England were placed in a group alongside Croatia, France and Switzerland. England beat the Croats 3–1 in August 2002, while the Swiss team are relatively inexperienced. Of course, France, who complete the group, will be difficult opponents, the England team is not afraid.

Two years ago, Eriksson said: "If you see our squad and the age of our players it looks good for 2004. The average age of a successful team is 28 or 29 and our players will have grown, gained experience and be stronger by Euro 2004." That moment has arrived.

Eriksson's squad is an exciting balance of players at the peak of their careers (David Beckham, Paul Scholes, Gary Neville, Nicky Butt, Sol Campbell and David James), players close to reaching their peak (Steven Gerrard and Michael Owen) and the youthful genius of Wayne Rooney.

There are some concerns on the horizon though. Sven has not had the chance to put a central defensive partnership to a long-term test; Gerrard has performed well on the left side of midfield, but a naturally left-footed player would give the team a better balance; and should Michael Owen succumb to injury, none of his deputies – Emile Heskey, James Beattie or Darius Vassell – can be completely relied upon to be as prolific as the Liverpool striker.

It is entirely normal for England to approach major championships on a wave of optimism, but this time there are real grounds to believe we could actually triumph in Portugal this summer and bring the trophy back to England for the first time in our history.

**Whether he starts or comes off the bench, midfield skillster Joe Cole is capable of causing problems for any defence.**

# SWITZERLAND

**They boast a gifted playmaker in Hakan Yakin and Alexander Frei is a proven international goalscorer, but will that be enough to get the Swiss rolling?**

**MANAGER**
**KOBI KUHN**
In 16 years as a player at FC Zurich, Kuhn won six Swiss league titles and five Swiss Cups, as well as amassing 63 international caps. The Swiss FA were persuaded to ditch their foreigner-only coach policy after witnessing Kuhn's good work with the Swiss Under-17 and Under-21 sides.

**ONE TO WATCH**
**ALEXANDER FREI**
While this 24-year-old striker has struggled to find goals for his French club side Rennes, he simply can't stop scoring for Switzerland. In only 22 internationals he has scored 14 goals, including crucial strikes against Ireland and Russia in the qualifiers.

## SWITZERLAND ESSENTIALS

◎ The headquarters of both of football's main governing bodies, UEFA and FIFA, are based in Switzerland.

◎ The highest honour the Swiss have won in international football is a silver medal at the 1924 Olympics in Paris.

## THE ROAD TO EURO 2004

**UEFA QUALIFYING GROUP 10**
08/09/02 v Georgia (h) won 4–1
12/10/02 v Albania (a) drew 1–1
16/10/02 v Rep of Ireland (a) won 2–1
02/04/03 v Georgia (a) drew 0–0
07/06/03 v Russia (h) drew 2–2
11/06/03 v Albania (h) won 3–2
10/09/03 v Russia (a) lost 1–4
11/10/03 v Rep of Ireland (h) won 2–0

**TOP SCORER**
Alexander Frei, 5 goals

**FINAL POSITION**

| P | W | D | L | F | A | GD | Pts | Psn |
|---|---|---|---|---|---|---|---|---|
| 8 | 4 | 3 | 1 | 15 | 11 | +4 | 15 | 1st |

**GROUP B FIXTURES**
13 June v Croatia, Leiria, 5pm
17 June v England, Coimbra, 5pm
21 June v France, Coimbra, 7.45pm

The Swiss have always been reluctant to entrust their national team to a native coach, traditionally preferring to appoint a foreigner, from Germany's Uli Stielike to England's Roy Hodgson. So it came as something of a surprise when for the first time in 12 years they gave the job to the Swiss Kobi Kuhn in the summer of 2001.

Two years later, Kuhn was being thrown in the air by his players after they had beaten Ireland in their final qualifying game in Basle to win their group and book a place at Portugal 2004.

"When a foreign coach comes in without any prior knowledge, there is never enough time to get to know the players," says the 60-year-old Kuhn. "But I helped the team find its own style of play and that means I don't have to worry too much about how our opponents play. We have a new generation of players coming through, who are trying to achieve one big aim."

That aim is a respectable showing at Euro 2004. However, this will be Switzerland's first major championship for eight years. They only have three experienced veterans from their Euro '96 squad – Stephane Henchoz, Johann Vogel and Stephane Chapuisat – so Kuhn is placing his faith in a new generation of Swiss players, many of whom he helped nurture during his spell as the national Under-17 and Under-21 coach.

In goal is the experienced Jorg Stiel, who plays behind a defence marshalled by Basle's Murat Yakin and Patrick Muller, while PSV Eindhoven's Johan Vogel operates in a midfield holding role.

The Swiss can be fluid attackers, with Richard Cabanas and Raphael Wicky pushing forward from midfield to join the wonderful Hakan Yakin, who plays just behind the forwards. English teams who have met Basle in Europe will know all about Yakin's qualities; he can score goals (three in the qualifiers) and create chances for others.

**Man between the sticks: Jorg Stiel.**

Up front, Alexander Frei and 35-year-old Stephane Chapuisat make up the Swiss striking partnership. Frei was a goalscoring revelation in the qualifiers, but he could do with more help from his senior partner. Chapuisat might be a Swiss legend, but his record of only 21 goals in 95 internationals indicates you can't rely on him for too many goals.

As they approached Euro 2004, the Swiss lost momentum. After throwing away a two-goal lead against Russia in June last year they never quite looked the same team, scraping past Albania 3–2, being thrashed by the Russians 4–1 and losing 2–1 to France in a friendly with a display Kuhn called "our worst of the year."

But you never know, and the English, French and Croats could all face a shock from Switzerland this summer.

# CROATIA

**The key players who helped Croatia to the 1998 World Cup semi-finals have retired and a new generation contribute to one of the meanest defences around**

**Croatia kept an impressive total of six clean sheets in 10 qualifiers.**

Croatia looked set to miss out on this summer's tournament after failing to win or even score in their first two qualifiers. In their opening game, the Croats could only manage a goalless draw at home to a poor Estonian side before being soundly beaten 2–0 by the Bulgarians in Sofia.

These results put Croatia's coach Otto Baric under pressure to resign; prominent coaches in the Croatian league criticised him for playing the wrong formations and said he lacked vision. Leading Croatian sports writer Tomislav Zidak declared, "Baric has deprived the team of guts and courage."

But it was just these qualities that helped spark a reversal in Croatia's fortunes as Baric expertly guided his team to second place in Group 8 with victories over Belgium, Andorra, Estonia and Belgium.

In the play-offs, Croatia were paired with Slovenia and were held to a 1–1 draw in the first leg at home. In the return match in Ljubljana, Baric made six changes, but it looked grim for the Croats when, with the score goalless, their leading defender Igor Tudor was sent off after an hour. However, instead of crumbling, within minutes Dado Prso had scored what would prove to be the tie's winner.

This is a new Croatia, almost unrecognisable from the side that reached the 1998 World Cup semi-finals in France. Zvonimir Boban, Alen Boksic, Davor Suker, Robert Jarni and Robert Prosinecki have all retired and been replaced with a younger set of players. "This is a new generation," says Chelsea's Mario Stanic. "The quality is there. Our back four is brilliant and teams are really going to find it difficult to break them down. We have five or six really good defenders who are ready to take care of anybody."

Stanic's confidence is justified after Croatia kept six clean sheets and conceded just four goals in their eight qualifiers. Goalkeeper Stipe Pletikosa was protected by a back four of Darijo Srna, a young right-back, hard to get past and a threat going forward, Josip Simunic at left-back, and the central partnership of Juventus' imperious Igor Tudor and Bayern Munich's Robert Kovac.

At the other end, the Croats are not exactly over flowing with goals. With the exception of their 4–0 win over Belgium, they didn't tend to dominate anyone in the qualifiers. The midfield quartet of Boris Zivkovic, Milan Rapaic, Giovani Rosso and Niko Kovac need to create more chances, while the striking partnership of Dado Prso and the quick Ivica Olic need to start scoring more consistently in Portugal.

**MANAGER**
**OTTO BARIC**

A native Croat known as "Herr Baric" for his long and distinguished career in Austrian football, which has included coaching the national side, winning the domestic title with VfB Admira Wacker Mödling, and taking both Rapid Vienna and SV Austria Salzburg to European finals. Baric succeeded Mirko Jozic after the 2002 World Cup.

**ONE TO WATCH**
**DADO PRSO**

The Monaco striker equalled a Champions League record by scoring four times against Deportivo La Coruna last autumn and was Croatia's hero in the play-off, scoring in both legs against Slovenia to claim a place at Euro 2004.

## CROATIA ESSENTIALS

◎ In 1903 Croatia lost their first 'international' games against Slavia Prague 15–0 and 20–0.

◎ Croatia didn't concede one goal during their four home games.

### THE ROAD TO EURO 2004

**UEFA QUALIFYING GROUP 8**

07/09/02 v Estonia (h) drew 0–0
12/10/02 v Bulgaria (a) lost 0–2
29/03/03 v Belgium (h) won 4–0
02/04/03 v Andorra (h) won 2–0
11/06/03 v Estonia (a) won 1–0
06/09/03 v Andorra (a) won 3–0
10/09/03 v Belgium (a) lost 1–2
11/10/03 v Bulgaria (h) won 1–0

**TOP SCORER**

Dado Prso, 3 goals

**FINAL POSITION**

| P | W | D | L | F | A | GD | Pts | Psn |
|---|---|---|---|---|---|---|---|---|
| 8 | 5 | 1 | 2 | 12 | 4 | +8 | 16 | 2nd |

**PLAY-OFFS**

15/11/03 v Slovenia (h) drew 1–1
19/11/03 v Slovenia (a) won 1–0

**GROUP B FIXTURES**

13 June v Switzerland, Leiria, 5pm
17 June v France, Leiria, 7.45pm
21 June v England, Lisbon, 7.45pm

# PORTUGAL EURO2004

## Your compact guide to Europe's premier international tournament

### GROUP A

| Date / Venue | Team | Score | Team | Score |
|---|---|---|---|---|
| 12 June, 5pm, Porto | PORTUGAL | 1 | GREECE | 2 |
| 12 June, 7.45pm, Faro-Loulé | SPAIN | 1 | RUSSIA | 0 |
| 16 June, 5pm, Porto | GREECE | 1 | SPAIN | 1 |
| 16 June, 7.45pm, Lisbon | RUSSIA | 0 | PORTUGAL | 2 |
| 20 June, 7.45pm, Faro-Loulé | RUSSIA | 2 | GREECE | 1 |
| 20 June, 7.45pm, Lisbon | SPAIN | 0 | PORTUGAL | 1 |

### GROUP B

| Date / Venue | Team | Score | Team | Score |
|---|---|---|---|---|
| 13 June, 5pm, Leiria | SWITZERLAND | 0 | CROATIA | 0 |
| 13 June, 7.45pm, Lisbon | FRANCE | 2 | ENGLAND | 1 |
| 17 June, 5pm, Coimbra | ENGLAND | 3 | SWITZERLAND | 0 |
| 17 June, 7.45pm, Leiria | CROATIA | 2 | FRANCE | 2 |
| 21 June, 7.45pm, Lisbon | CROATIA | 2 | ENGLAND | 4 |
| 21 June, 7.45pm, Coimbra | SWITZERLAND | 1 | FRANCE | 3 |

### GROUP C

| Date / Venue | Team | Score | Team | Score |
|---|---|---|---|---|
| 14 June, 5pm, Guimarães | DENMARK | 0 | ITALY | 0 |
| 14 June, 7.45pm, Lisbon | SWEDEN | 5 | BULGARIA | 0 |
| 18 June, 5pm, Braga | BULGARIA | 0 | DENMARK | 2 |
| 18 June, 7.45pm, Porto | ITALY | 1 | SWEDEN | 1 |
| 22 June, 7.45pm, Guimarães | ITALY | 2 | BULGARIA | 1 |
| 22 June, 7.45pm, Porto | DENMARK | 2 | SWEDEN | 2 |

### GROUP D

| Date / Venue | Team | Score | Team | Score |
|---|---|---|---|---|
| 15 June, 5pm, Aveiro | CZECH REP | 2 | LATVIA | 1 |
| 15 June, 7.45pm, Porto | GERMANY | 1 | HOLLAND | 1 |
| 19 June, 5pm, Porto | LATVIA | 0 | GERMANY | 0 |
| 19 June, 7.45pm, Aveiro | HOLLAND | 2 | CZECH REP | 3 |
| 23 June, 7.45pm, Braga | HOLLAND | 3 | LATVIA | 0 |
| 23 June, 7.45pm, Lisbon | GERMANY | 1 | CZECH REP | 2 |

All match times BST

# EURO 2004 FIXTURES

## QUARTER-FINAL #1

24 June, 7.45pm, Lisbon

**WINNER GROUP A V RUNNER-UP GROUP B**

Aet: Portugal win 6-5 on Penalties

2 — 2

## QUARTER-FINAL #2

25 June, 7.45, Lisbon

**WINNER GROUP B V RUNNER-UP GROUP A**

0 — 1

## QUARTER-FINAL #3

26 June, 7.45pm, Faro-Loulé

**WINNER GROUP C V RUNNER-UP GROUP D**

Aet: Holland win 6-5 on Penalties

0 — 0

## QUARTER-FINAL #4

27 June, 7.45pm, Porto

**WINNER GROUP D V RUNNER-UP GROUP C**

3 — 0

## SEMI-FINAL #1

30 June, 7.45pm, José Alvalade, Lisbon

**WINNER OF QUARTER-FINAL #1 V WINNER OF QUARTER-FINAL #3**

2 — 1

## SEMI-FINAL #2

1 July, 7.45pm, Dragão, Porto

**WINNER OF QUARTER-FINAL #2 V WINNER OF QUARTER-FINAL #4**

1 — 0

## EURO 2004 FINAL

4 July 7.45pm, Luz, Lisbon

**WINNER OF SEMI-FINAL #1 V WINNER OF SEMI-FINAL #2**

0 — 1

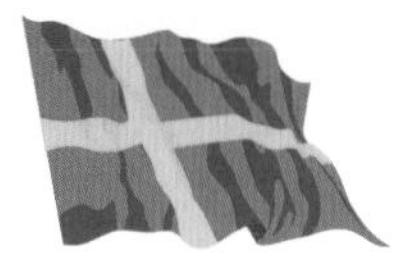

# SWEDEN

**Qualifying form suggests that the Swedes should reach the latter stages, but what was that about damned lies and statistics?**

**MANAGER**
**TOMMY SODERBERG AND LARS LAGERBACK**
"Four eyes are better than two" says Tommy Soderberg on why his partnership with Lars Lagerback works so well for Sweden. Soderberg is the more experienced having coached AIK Solna and Djürgardens IF, and has worked with Lagerback for the national side since 1997. Soderberg has announced he will step aside after Euro 2004 and leave Lagerback in sole charge.

**ONE TO WATCH**
**ZLATAN IBRAHIMOVIC**
The supremely-talented Ajax striker will be hoping to repeat his prolific form from the Dutch league at Euro 2004. The skilful 22-year-old has long been talked about as having the potential to be one of the best strikers in Europe.

## SWEDEN ESSENTIALS

- Sweden hosted the European Championship in 1992 and reached the semi-finals, their best ever showing in the tournament.
- Sweden's 1–0 defeat to Latvia in the qualifiers was their first competitive loss at home since 1997.

### THE ROAD TO EURO 2004

**UEFA QUALIFYING GROUP 2**
07/09/02 v Latvia (a) drew 0–0
12/10/02 v Hungary (h) drew 1–1
02/04/03 v Hungary (a) won 2–1
07/06/03 v San Marino (a) won 6–0
11/06/03 v Poland (h) won 3–0
06/09/03 v San Marino (h) won 5–0
10/09/03 v Poland (a) won 2–0
11/10/03 v Latvia (h) lost 0–1

**TOP SCORER**
Marcus Allback, 5 goals

**FINAL POSITION**

| P | W | D | L | F | A | GD | Pts | Psn |
|---|---|---|---|---|---|---|---|---|
| 8 | 5 | 2 | 1 | 19 | 3 | +16 | 17 | 1st |

**GROUP C FIXTURES**
14 June v Bulgaria, Lisbon, 7.45pm
18 June v Italy, Porto, 7.45pm
22 June v Denmark, Porto, 7.45pm

At first glance Sweden appear to have a genuine chance of winning Euro 2004. They were group winners in qualifying, losing just once in eight games, while scoring 19 goals and conceding only three. This is the form of a team who should harbour serious ambitions of being in Lisbon on 4 July to contest the Final.

**Without the prematurely retired Henrik Larsson, where will the goals come from for the Swedes?**

But are things really that simple for Sweden? If you take a closer look, all their wins were achieved in a group containing teams that were either young or in transition, and certainly not the strongest opposition: Poland, Hungary, Latvia and San Marino. Outside of that, Sweden could only score at an average of a goal a game. Also worth bearing in mind is their wretched form in friendlies over the last year, which has seen them lose to fellow Euro 2004 finalists Greece, Portugal and Croatia, as well as Tunisia and Egypt.

Drawn in Group C alongside Bulgaria, Denmark and Italy, it appears as though there will be a grand Scandinavian battle for the runners-up spot behind the Italians.

"It is certainly tough for us," says Sweden's joint coach Lars Lagerback. "This is a very even group and we will need three good days if we are to advance."

It is the Swedish defence who really need to perform on these days. As individuals they are unexceptional defenders, who play their club football at such modest outfits as AIK Solna, Southampton and Heerenveen, but as a unit they form an almost impenetrable barrier. In goal is Andreas Isaksson, who took over from Magnus Hedman during the qualifying campaign and kept four cleans sheets, while in front of him is a back four of Olof Mellberg, Michael Svensson, Erik Edman and Teddy Lucic.

While the Swedes can claim a solid midfield, often enlivened by the creativity of Freddie Ljungberg, it is in attack that they have some development to make. They have never really recovered from the premature international retirement of Henrik Larsson. The Celtic striker made a one-game comeback in the qualifiers, but has since confirmed he will not be at Euro 2004, and even a pleading letter from the Swedish president of UEFA Lennart Johansson failed to alter his decision.

So it looks as if Sweden will have to make do with the uninspiring Marcus Allback (who has so far failed to make an impression at Aston Villa), Mattias Jonson (who ended six years without an international goal last year) and their one source of hope, Ajax's promising Zlatan Ibrahimovic, in their search for goals. One of these strikers needs to find some form if the Swedes are to triumph in their group stage mini-battle with the Danes.

# BULGARIA

**Manager Plamen Markov was plucked from obscurity, but he revitalised the Bulgarian team and led them to Portugal 2004**

**Bulgarian Footballer of the Year and top scorer in qualification, Dimitar Berbatov.**

There was a palpable sense of disbelief when Plamen Markov was handed the task of reviving Bulgarian football in December 2001. In the wake of the country's failure to reach both Euro 2000 and the 2002 World Cup, it was expected the Bulgarian FA would turn to a more experienced coach, but Markov, who had never even coached in the Bulgarian top flight was given the job.

"Giving this important job to a second division coach is a real risk," declared the former Bulgarian manager Dimitar Penev. "Our football authorities will have to take full responsibility for what happens."

Two years later they were more than happy to do that after watching Markov lead Bulgaria into the Euro 2004 finals.

After Bulgaria had been trounced 6–0 by the Czech Republic in the last World Cup qualifiers, Markov decided to place his faith in an emerging group of young players and was rewarded by a qualifying campaign which saw them overcome Belgium and Croatia to make it to Portugal as group winners.

"Not long ago there was a lot of apathy and only 1,500 supporters watching us, but now we have a new stadium and we get 40,000 for every game," says Celtic's Stilian Petrov. "Our success in the qualifying group is rated bigger than our performance at the 1994 World Cup when we reached the semi-finals. We have a young team, but we can cause a few surprises at Euro 2004."

Bulgarian legend Hristo Stoichkov has said that his country's progress at the Championship finals will depend on the performances of three players – Stilian Petrov, Martin Petrov (no relation) and Dimitar Berbatov.

The two Petrovs pull the strings in midfield; Stilian, with his vision and ability to carry the ball forward, and Martin, who plays in the Bundesliga at Wolfsburg, with his runs along the left wing. Relying on their service up front is Dimitar Berbatov, who scored five goals in qualifying to take his overall record for Bulgaria to an impressive 15 goals in 25 appearances.

While this Bulgarian team has an average age of just 24, there are also some old hands around to offer guidance such as Marian Hristov from Kaiserslautern, 1860 Munich's Daniel Borimirov and Dynamo Kiev's Georgi Peev.

Youthful exuberance was enough to get Bulgaria to Euro 2004, but it could still prove to be their weakness this summer, and it will be very hard work for the team to lift themselves out of what is one of the toughest groups, containing strong opposition in the shape of Italy, Sweden and Denmark.

**MANAGER**
**PLAMEN MARKOV**

Markov enjoyed a decorated career as a player, winning 34 caps for Bulgaria and being part of the renowned CSKA Sofia side, which won five national titles in the late Seventies and early Eighties. Before being unexpectedly handed the national job, Markov was coach of Grenoble in France, and Chardaton Gabroro, FC Minion and Vidima Rakovski in Bulgaria.

**ONE TO WATCH**
**DIMITAR BERBATOV**

This tall and strong 23-year-old striker is the current Bulgarian Footballer of the Year. Berbatov plays his club football in Germany for Bayer Leverkusen and scored against Manchester United in the Champions League last season.

## BULGARIA ESSENTIALS

- Plamen Markov banned his players from having sex ahead of their Euro 2004 qualifier against Belgium. "I need all their energies concentrated on this game," he said. His policy didn't work that well – they drew 2–2.
- This is Bulgaria's first appearance in the European Championship since 1996.

### THE ROAD TO EURO 2004

**UEFA QUALIFYING GROUP 8**

07/09/02 v Belgium (a) won 2–0
12/10/02 v Croatia (h) won 2–0
16/10/02 v Andorra (h) won 2–1
02/04/03 v Estonia (a) drew 0–0
07/06/03 v Belgium (h) drew 2–2
06/09/03 v Estonia (h) won 2–0
10/09/03 v Andorra (a) won 3–0
11/10/03 v Croatia (a) lost 0–1

**TOP SCORER**

Dimitar Berbatov, 5 goals

**FINAL POSITION**

| P | W | D | L | F | A | GD | Pts | Psn |
|---|---|---|---|---|---|---|---|---|
| 8 | 5 | 2 | 1 | 13 | 4 | +9 | 17 | 1st |

**GROUP C FIXTURES**

14 June v Sweden, Lisbon, 7.45pm
18 June v Denmark, Braga, 5pm
22 June v Italy, Guimaraes, 7.45pm

# DENMARK

**With a solid defence, the quickest winger in the world and accomplished strikers to put the chances away, Denmark will be formidable opponents for anyone**

**MANAGER**
**MORTEN OLSEN**
Since succeeding Bo Johansen in the autumn of 2000, Morten Olsen has restored Danish pride by qualifying for the 2002 World Cup finals and now Euro 2004. Olsen amassed 102 international caps for Denmark before establishing himself as a coach by winning national titles with Brondby in Denmark and Ajax in Holland.

**ONE TO WATCH**
**MARTIN JORGENSEN**
England know all about this Danish midfielder after his match-winning performance in which he scored two goals against them at Old Trafford last November. Jorgensen has been doing the same in Serie A with Udinese for the last seven seasons, and at 28 years old, should be approaching his peak.

## DENMARK ESSENTIALS

◎ The 15 goals Denmark scored in their qualifying campaign were shared out between 10 of their players and one own goal.

◎ Denmark qualified for Euro '92, which they went on to win, as late replacements for Yugoslavia, who were forced to withdraw because of the country's war.

### THE ROAD TO EURO 2004

**UEFA QUALIFYING GROUP 2**
07/09/02 v Norway (a) drew 2–2
12/10/02 v Lux'bourg (h) won 2–0
29/03/03 v Romania (a) won 5–2
02/04/03 v Bosnia-H (h) lost 0–2
07/06/03 v Norway (h) won 1–0
11/06/03 v Lux'bourg (a) won 2–0
10/09/03 v Romania (h) drew 2–2
11/10/03 v Bosnia-H (a) drew 1–1

**TOP SCORER**
Jon Dahl Tomasson, 3 goals

**FINAL POSITION**

| P | W | D | L | F | A | GD | Pts | Psn |
|---|---|---|---|---|---|---|---|---|
| 8 | 4 | 3 | 1 | 15 | 9 | +6 | 15 | 1st |

**GROUP C FIXTURES**
14 June v Italy, Guimaraes, 5pm
18 June v Bulgaria, Braga, 5pm
22 June v Sweden, Porto, 7.45pm

Denmark might not be one of the favourites to win Euro 2004, but no-one will be underestimating them this summer. Certainly not France, who were comprehensively beaten by the Danes at the last World Cup; and not England, who suffered a 3–2 defeat to them in a friendly at Old Trafford last November.

While Denmark cannot claim to have a superstar like Peter Schmeichel or Brian Laudrup, who were both part of the Danish team that won the European Championship in 1992, Morten Olsen has constructed a sturdy team who have only lost two competitive games in the last four years.

"We are not Brazil, but we keep qualifying for these tournaments, which is a great achievement for a small country," says the Danish captain Rene Henriksen. "I would say there are four really good nations in European football now, but we are in the group just below that and can really cause a few surprises."

Denmark will always be difficult to beat with a defensive unit that can boast Aston Villa's Thomas Sorensen in goal and a back four of Thomas Helveg, Henriksen, Martin Laursen and Niclas Jensen. Just for extra protection, the Premiership pair of Thomas Gravesen and Claus Jensen form another barrier in front of them.

But don't be fooled into thinking Denmark are a dour side. Morten Olsen uses an attacking 4–3–3 formation to take advantage of having a surplus of fast and skilful wingers in his squad. He can take his pick from Chelsea's Jesper Gronkjaer, PSV Eindhoven's Dennis Rommedahl (who can run 100 metres in 10.2 seconds!), Peter Lovenkrands of Rangers and Martin Jorgensen from the Italian side Udinese.

The responsibility for putting away the chances created by this midfield falls to the partnership of Ebbe Sand and Jon Dahl Tomasson, who have scored nearly half a century of international goals between them. Newcastle fans are still baffled by how Tomasson has changed from the woeful player they watched at St James' Park six years ago into a highly prolific striker, who was second top scorer at the 2002 World Cup and helped AC Milan win the Champions League last season. His partner, Schalke's Ebbe Sand has been enduring a lean time in front of goal of late, but has the class to come good in Portugal this summer.

Olsen says he wants his team to play a style of football that "aims to please the eye and be effective at the same time". He certainly has the players to do that, but it would still be a major surprise if it carried them any further than the quarter-finals this summer.

**Udinese's Martin Jorgensen is just one of a crop of quick and skilful Denmark wingers.**

# ITALY

**The Euro 2000 finalists have endured some indifferent results in recent years, but a new commitment to attack has transformed their Portugal 2004 prospects**

**Francesco Totti is one of the Italian attackers benefiting from coach Trapattoni's more adventurous approach.**

The calls for Giovanni Trapattoni to resign in the aftermath of Italy's shock defeat to Wales in a Euro 2004 qualifier in the autumn of 2002 were deafening. Following so soon after the humiliation of losing to South Korea at the World Cup, Italian football was plunged into despair.

"In 2002, we've lost to the Czechs, to Croatia and South Korea, to Slovenia and Wales; we've only been able to beat Ecuador and Azerbaijan," declared one of the leading Italian sports papers *Corriere dello Sport*. "Wherever the Italian federation president is today, whatever he's doing, please liberate us from this endless nightmare."

But these calls were not heeded and instead Italy's most successful ever club coach remained in the job, where he used all his experience to purge his players of their self-doubt and restore some pride. Italy remained unbeaten in their next five Euro 2004 qualifiers, winning four of them, including a cathartic 4–0 victory over the Welsh in Milan, to finish as group winners.

The catalyst for this stunning turnaround was Trapattoni's decision to dump his (in)famously defensive tactics. As the Welsh discovered, the Italians now play with as many as three strikers and are not content to merely sit on a one-goal lead any more. The attacking forces of Francesco Totti, Christian Vieri, Filippo Inzahgi and Alessandro Del Piero were finally unleashed, and together they scored all but two of Italy's 17 goals in the qualifying campaign.

This new approach has not been at the expense of Italy's traditionally miserly defence. In Juventus' goalkeeper Gianluigi Buffon, and the central defensive partnership of AC Milan's Alessandro Nesta and Inter Milan's Fabio Cannavaro, Italy arguably have the best back line of any team in Portugal. Even more worryingly for Europe's strikers, Trapattoni has not given up trying to persuade the legendary Paolo Maldini to make a comeback this summer.

If the Italians have a weakness, it is undoubtedly in midfield. While they possess plenty of steely grafters such as Gennaro Gattuso, Alessio Tacchinardi, Simone Perrotta and Mauro Camoranesi, they lack a more creative midfielder and wingers.

The Azzurri were just minutes from winning Euro 2000, and having survived a difficult qualification, they now believe they can go one better this summer.

"When we're in form, no-one can stop us," says Nesta. "In 2002 we threw away a chance to win the World Cup too, so we will make sure we make up for this in Portugal."

**MANAGER**
**GIOVANNI TRAPATTONI**

Giovanni Trapattoni finally became coach of Italy in the summer of 2000. Before that he had won just about everything in football. At Juventus, he claimed six Scudettos, the European Cup, the Cup-Winners' Cup, the Super Cup, two Italian Cups and the Intercontinental Cup. At Inter Milan he won another Scudetto and the UEFA Cup, and then the German title with Bayern Munich.

**ONE TO WATCH**
**ANTONIO CASSANO**

In the summer of 2001, Cassano became the world's most expensive teenager when Roma paid £19 million for him. Early on, he struggled, but the 21-year-old striker has been in fine form this season and was rewarded with his first international appearance against Poland last November.

## ITALY ESSENTIALS

- Italy have twice failed to qualify for the European Championships in the last 20 years, in 1984 and 1992.
- Italy boss Giovanni Trapattoni keeps a bottle of holy water in his jacket pocket during games.

### THE ROAD TO EURO 2004

**UEFA QUALIFYING GROUP 9**

07/09/02 v Azerbaijan (a) won 2–0
12/10/02 v Serbia & M (h) drew 1–1
16/10/02 v Wales (a) lost 1–2
29/03/03 v Finland (h) won 2–0
11/06/03 v Finland (a) won 2–0
06/09/03 v Wales (h) won 4–0
10/09/03 v Serbia & M (a) drew 1–1
11/10/03 v Azerbaijan (h) won 4–0

**TOP SCORER**

Filippo Inzaghi, 6 goals

**FINAL POSITION**

| P | W | D | L | F | A | GD | Pts | Psn |
|---|---|---|---|---|---|---|---|---|
| 8 | 5 | 2 | 1 | 17 | 4 | +13 | 17 | 1st |

**GROUP C FIXTURES**

14 June v Denmark, Guimaraes, 5pm
18 June v Sweden, Porto, 7.45pm
22 June v Bulgaria, Guimaraes, 7.45pm

# CZECH REPUBLIC

**Awesome in qualifying and with one of the potential stars of the tournament in Pavel Nedved, the Czech Republic look set for a successful Euro 2004**

**MANAGER**
**KAREL BRUCKNER**
The 64-year-old coach has never worked outside the former Czechoslovakia, spending his career in charge of ASK Inter Bratislava, SK Sigma Olmouc, FK Drnovice and now the national team. Bruckner looked after the national Under-23 side at the 2000 Olympics and the Under-21 side before being awarded the senior job.

**ONE TO WATCH**
**TOMAS ROSICKY**
The skilful Czech midfielder came through the youth ranks of Sparta Prague before being snapped up by Borussia Dortmund for a record German transfer fee of £8 million in January 2001. After an initial quiet spell, the 23-year-old has been living up to the hype over the last couple of seasons.

## CZECH REPUBLIC ESSENTIALS

◎ The only team to stop the Czech Republic winning en route to Euro 2004 was Holland, who held them to a 1–1 draw in March 2003.

◎ Karel Poborsky became the Czech Republic's joint most capped player at the end of 2003 when he played his 90th international.

### THE ROAD TO EURO 2004

**UEFA QUALIFYING GROUP 2**

12/10/02 v Moldova (a) won 2–0
16/10/02 v Belarus (h) won 2–0
29/03/03 v Holland (a) drew 1–1
02/04/03 v Austria (h) won 4–0
11/06/03 v Moldova (h) won 5–0
06/09/03 v Belarus (a) won 3–1
10/09/03 v Holland (h) won 3–1
11/10/03 v Austria (a) won 3–2

**TOP SCORER**

Jan Koller, 6 goals

**FINAL POSITION**

| P | W | D | L | F | A | GD | Pts | Psn |
|---|---|---|---|---|---|---|---|---|
| 8 | 7 | 1 | 0 | 23 | 5 | +18 | 22 | 1st |

**GROUP D FIXTURES**

15 June v Latvia, Aveiro, 5pm
19 June v Holland, Aveiro, 7.45pm
23 June v Germany, Lisbon, 7.45pm

In autumn 2001 the Czech Republic were coming to terms with their second successive failure to reach the World Cup finals on the back of a winless trip to Euro 2000. How times change. Now, less than two years later, the Czechs are looking forward to this summer's tournament on the back of an unbeaten run of 19 games.

The architect of this extraordinary revival is their former national Under-21 coach Karel Bruckner, who succeeded Jozef Chovanec as coach in December 2001. Bruckner brought several young players with him and by moulding them together with the older generation he has produced a side with the potential to go all the way at Euro 2004.

The Czechs were simply awesome in their qualifying campaign, remaining unbeaten with a record of seven wins and one draw. Bruckner's side scored at a rate of nearly three goals a game, and only the defending champions France scored more. At the back, the Czechs conceded a mere five goals in eight games. It is with good reason Pavel Nedved says this is the best Czech team for over a quarter of a century.

Nedved himself is the Czechs' most potent weapon. At 30, he is a player at his peak, who regularly turns in superb displays for Juventus in the Champions League. If Nedved finds his best form he could inspire the rest of the team all the way to the final.

Surrounding Nedved in midfield is a wealth of talent. Karel Poborsky may have been a figure of ridicule during his time at Manchester United, but he has since rediscovered his stunning Euro '96 form. Complementing this pair is the flair of Borussia Dortmund's Tomas Rosicky and the experience of Ajax's Tomas Galasek.

Up front for the Czechs is Borussia Dortmund's towering six foot seven inch striker Jan Koller, who scored six goals in the qualifying games. When he's not scoring, he is laying on chances for his partner, Liverpool's Milan Baros.

Borussia Dortmund's skilful midfielder Tomas Rosicky is one to watch this summer.

There is one note of caution for the Czechs. They made it to Euro 2000 on a similar wave of optimism after remaining unbeaten in their qualifiers, but they didn't do well at all in the Low Countries and scuttled home early without a win. A better and more experienced side should stick around a lot longer this time.

# LATVIA

**Once ranked down with the likes of Guatemala in the world rankings, Latvia's Euro 2004 qualification is one of the most heart-warming stories of the competition**

**Maris Verpakovskis: expect to see this striker in the Premiership one day.**

A year ago Latvia wouldn't have dared to dream about playing at this summer's European Championship. The president of the Baltic country's football federation, Guntis Indriksons, complained about how hard it was to find 11 players to play for their national team as they only had around 100 players to choose from.

This meant Latvia could be found in the lower reaches of FIFA's world rankings alongside Guatemala and New Zealand. They had never even come close to qualifying for a major championship, and in their attempt to make it to the 2002 World Cup they finished fourth in their group and suffered the embarrassment of being held to a draw by San Marino.

Manager Aleksandrs Starkovs was insistent that his country had the players to reach a tournament if they simply changed their approach from playing to avoid defeat to playing to win. This new approach could be seen when Latvia kicked off their qualifying campaign with a hard-fought draw against Sweden. They followed up with a win over Poland and home and away wins over San Marino.

Even consecutive defeats to Poland and Hungary couldn't undermine their new resolve and they secured a play-off berth with a 3–1 win over Hungary followed by a 1–0 win in Sweden, which ended their hosts' 25-game unbeaten run in qualifiers.

An unsuspecting Turkey couldn't hide their delight at being drawn against Latvia in the play-offs. Turkish football federation president Haluk Ulusoy declared: "When you look at where Turkey is right now, it cannot be compared with Latvia." But the Latvians won the first leg 1–0 in Riga, and then booked their place at Euro 2004 after coming back from two goals down to claim a 2–2 draw in Turkey.

The success of this historic campaign was based on Starkovs' wily counter-attacking approach to games. This involved a defence including former Crystal Palace goalkeeper Aleksandrs Kolinko and the Arsenal defender Igors Stepanovs soaking up the opposition's attacks before breaking forward at pace to feed the prolific Maris Verpakovskis, who scored twice against Turkey in the two play-off games.

"The next step is to try to be very solid in the finals," says the former Fulham striker Andrejs Stolcers. "I heard people predicting we will lose by five-nil and six-nil, but we don't want that."

It is highly unlikely this will happen, but the Latvians have been dealt a cruel draw by being placed in a group alongside Holland, Germany and the Czech Republic – but people hardly expected them to qualify or even win their play-off either.

### MANAGER ALEKSANDRS STARKOVS

A prolific goalscorer for Daugava Riga in his playing days, Starkovs was the first Latvian to score over 100 goals in the Soviet Union's top flight. As a coach, he led Skonto Riga to an incredible 11 successive league titles before being appointed national coach in May 2001.

### ONE TO WATCH MARIS VERPAKOVSKIS

The Skonto Riga striker scored six goals in the qualifiers, once had an unsuccessful trial at Wolves, but should now have no trouble earning a lucrative move abroad.

## LATVIA ESSENTIALS

◎ Football is only the fourth most popular sport in Latvia behind ice hockey, basketball and athletics.

◎ Latvia gained its independence from the Soviet Union as recently as 1991, so this was only their third attempt to qualify for the European Championship.

### THE ROAD TO EURO 2004

**UEFA QUALIFYING GROUP 4**

07/09/02 v Sweden (h) drew 0–0
12/10/02 v Poland (a) won 1–0
20/11/02 v San Marino (a) won 1–0
30/04/03 v San Marino (h) won 3–0
07/06/03 v Hungary (a) lost 1–3
06/09/03 v Poland (h) lost 0–2
10/09/03 v Hungary (h) won 3–1
11/10/03 v Sweden (a) won 1–0

**TOP SCORER**

Maris Verpakovskis, 6 goals

**FINAL POSITION**

| P | W | D | L | F | A | GD | Pts | Psn |
|---|---|---|---|---|---|---|---|---|
| 8 | 5 | 1 | 2 | 10 | 6 | +4 | 16 | 2nd |

**PLAY-OFFS**

15/11/03 v Turkey (h) won 1–0
19/11/03 v Turkey (a) drew 2–2

**GROUP D FIXTURES**

15 June v Czech Rep, Aveiro, 5pm
19 June v Germany, Porto, 5pm
23 June v Holland, Braga, 7.45pm

# GERMANY

**Are the Germans too reliant on Michael Ballack? Do they score enough goals? Will they win the competition anyway?!**

**MANAGER**
**RUDI VOELLER**
A legend as a player, Voeller scored 47 goals in 90 international appearances and was a leading member of their World Cup winning side of 1990. For four years after retiring in 1996, Voeller stayed out of coaching until Germany approached him about the national job. He has since led them to the World Cup final and now Euro 2004.

**ONE TO WATCH**
**KEVIN KURANYI**
Manchester United learned about Kuranyi when he tore them apart and scored in Stuttgart's 2–1 win over them in the Champions League last year. The 21-year-old, who made his international debut against Iceland in the qualifiers, is tall, quick and difficult to mark.

## GERMANY ESSENTIALS

◎ Germany have been crowned champions of Europe on three occasions, 1972, 1980 and 1996.

◎ Germany were the first team to win the European Championship by scoring a "golden goal" when they beat the Czech Republic at Wembley in 1996.

### THE ROAD TO EURO 2004

**UEFA QUALIFYING GROUP 5**
07/09/02 v Lithuania (a) won 2–0
16/10/02 v Faroe Islands (h) won 2–1
29/03/03 v Lithuania (h) drew 1–1
07/06/03 v Scotland (a) drew 1–1
11/06/03 v Faroe Islands (a) won 2–0
06/09/03 v Iceland (a) drew 0–0
10/09/03 v Scotland (h) won 2–1
11/10/03 v Iceland (h) won 3–0

**TOP SCORERS**
Michael Ballack and
Fredi Bobic, 5 goals

**FINAL POSITION**

| P | W | D | L | F | A | GD | Pts | Psn |
|---|---|---|---|---|---|---|---|---|
| 8 | 5 | 3 | 0 | 13 | 4 | +9 | 18 | 1st |

**GROUP D FIXTURES**
15 June v Holland, Porto, 7.45pm
19 June v Latvia, Porto, 5pm
23 June v Czech Rep, Lisbon 7.45pm

Germany might have booked their place at Euro 2004 without losing a game, but throughout the last 18 months a great army of critics at home have dismissed them as an ordinary team with no hope of success this summer.

Of course, all this has a familiar ring to it. Exactly the same was said about the Germans on the eve of the last World Cup finals. Only for Rudi Voeller to promptly lead his team all the way to the final, where they were beaten by two goals from Ronaldo.

Writing off Germany is always a foolish thing to do. The dogged mentality of the German player is built for major championships, and over the last two decades, they have reached the final game of four World Cups and two European Championships. "Pressure situations bring out the best in us," says German centre-half Christian Worns. "I'm convinced we are ready for the challenge."

Such optimism is based upon the German's impressive defence. Oliver Kahn is arguably still the best goalkeeper in the world, while Worns has become a top-class centre half and he leads a defence that also boasts Marko Rehmer, Arne Friedrich and Christoph Metzelder. Together, they let just four goals past them in qualifying.

Then there is Michael Ballack. As the Bayern Munich midfielder proved at the last World Cup, he is an inspirational figure who can drag a team along with him. Alongside Ballack in the centre of the field is the excellent Jens Jeremies, whose holding role allows his club team-mate the freedom to get forward.

However, the Germans do have their problems. They didn't lose in qualifying, but they never really managed any convincing wins either, against Scotland, Lithuania and the Faroe Islands. When exposed to stronger teams in friendlies over the last year, the Germans have lost to Holland, Italy and Spain.

**Oliver Kahn: probably the best goalkeeper in the world.**

German legend Franz Beckenbauer has constantly warned that this team are over-reliant on Ballack, who by the end of last year had scored 14 goals in 36 appearances. An injury to him could effectively derail Germany's challenge.

Goals are another cause for concern after Germany only managed 13 in the qualifiers, and even the Faroe Islands restricted them to just two in each of their games. "This has been a deficiency in the team and it is something we must work on," says Rudi Voeller. At least one from Miroslav Klose, Oliver Neuville, Kevin Kuranyi and Fredi Bobic need to take more responsibility for goals.

To make matters worse for the Germans, they have been drawn in the tournament's most difficult group. It looks as though it will be difficult for them to get past the first round, but it is worth repeating: never underestimate the Germans at a major championship.

# HOLLAND

**With a dazzling array of talent from front to back, Holland can win the tournament if (and it's a big 'if') their players remain united this summer**

**Dutch goalscoring legend Patrick Kluivert may be fighting Ruud van Nistelrooy for a starting place.**

In their play-off games against Scotland, the Dutch perfectly showcased the two sides to their character. In the first leg at Hampden Park, they were sloppy, indecisive and didn't look like a team. They lost 1–0. Four days later in the deciding leg at the Amsterdam Arena they were unified, competitive and clinical. They won 6–0.

"It's our drama," says the former Dutch coach Leo Beenhakker. "With all our talent, our technical and tactical skills, our offensive football, we have only won one major tournament. We are like a boxer who boxes very well but doesn't have a knock-out. We don't have the mentality to take him by the throat. We have no killer touch. That's been our problem during the whole history of our football."

Other than winning the European Championship 16 years ago, the Dutch have only succeeded in becoming the nearly men of European football. They lost in the World Cup final in 1974 and 1978, and in more recent times, lost on penalties in the semi-finals of the 1998 World Cup and the last European Championship.

Will the Dutch be any different this summer? There is no doubt that they have the individual talent to overcome any opponent and actually win Euro 2004, but their success hinges on whether their players can remain united and play as a team for a month.

Former national coach Louis van Gaal is not optimistic:

"I don't think these players have the right spirit and ambition to play for the national team."

It is often said that the Dutch have too many big names in their squad, too many egos struggling for recognition. And you can see why with a look at the players at Dick Advocaat's disposal, which reads like a who's who of world football. Keeping it tight at the back are Edwin van der Sar in goal, and a defence of Michael Reiziger, Jaap Stam (whose brilliant performances continue to expose Manchester United's error in selling him), Frank de Boer and Giovanni van Bronckhorst.

In midfield, there is an abundance of talent, but they are not without their problems. Edgar Davids, Marc Overmars, Clarence Seedorf and Philip Cocu are all wonderful players, but there is a fear they might now be past their best as well. They have been bolstered by the introduction of Andy van der Meyde, Mark van Bommel and Wesley Sneijder. Ajax's Rafael van der Vaart is deployed just in front of the midfield in the classic number 10 role.

The Dutch have an embarrassment of riches up front. Advocaat can call on the leading goalscorers from last season's Premiership, Manchester United's Ruud van Nistelrooy, last season's La Liga, Roy Makaay (now with Bayern Munich), and the most prolific goalscorer in the history of the Holland side, Patrick Kluivert. During qualification, Advocaat stated that Van Nistelrooy and Kluivert can't play together so the only problem is knowing who to start with, but it appears as though it will be Van Nistelrooy after his hat-trick against the Scots in the play-offs.

### MANAGER
**DICK ADVOCAAT**

The experienced Advocaat is currently in his second spell as Dutch coach. In his first one in the early Nineties he took Holland to the 1994 World Cup quarter-finals in the USA. He was recalled to the national team to replace Louis van Gaal in the autumn of 2002.

### ONE TO WATCH
**RAFAEL VAN DER VAART**

The 21-year-old Ajax midfielder's influence clearly grew on Holland during the qualifying campaign. He scored three goals and looks to have now made the withdrawn striker role behind either Van Nistelrooy or Kluivert his own.

## HOLLAND ESSENTIALS

- By the end of 2003, Dick Advocaat's record in his two spells as Dutch coach was played 36, won 23, drawn eight and lost six.
- The Dutch had the best qualifying record of all 10 teams in the Euro 2004 play-offs.

### THE ROAD TO EURO 2004

**UEFA QUALIFYING GROUP 3**

07/09/02 v Belarus (h) won 3–0
16/10/02 v Austria (a) won 3–0
29/03/03 v Czech Rep (h) drew 1–1
02/04/03 v Moldova (a) won 2–1
07/06/03 v Belarus (a) won 2–0
06/09/03 v Austria (h) won 3–1
10/09/03 v Czech Rep (a) lost 1–3
11/10/03 v Moldova (h) won 5–0

**FINAL POSITION**

| P | W | D | L | F | A | GD | Pts | Psn |
|---|---|---|---|---|---|---|---|---|
| 8 | 6 | 1 | 1 | 20 | 6 | +14 | 19 | 2nd |

**PLAY-OFFS**

15/11/03 v Scotland (a) lost 0–1
19/11/03 v Scotland (h) won 6–0

**TOP SCORER**

Ruud van Nistelrooy, 5 goals

**GROUP D FIXTURES**

15 June v Germany, Porto, 7.45pm
19 June v Czech Rep, Aveiro, 7.45pm
23 June v Latvia, Braga, 7.45pm

# WHEN FOOTBALL CAME HOME

**Even though our lads couldn't quite end 30 years of hurt when England hosted Euro '96, the tournament was a memorable carnival of football...**

ALAN SHEARER SURGES INTO THE German box and whips the ball across the face of goal. At the far post a blond-haired, red-faced Gazza, his unfamiliar grey kit drenched in sweat, powers in for one last thrust for victory. The ball beats the outstretched arm of Kopke and the German goal is wide open. For an instant time stands still. The whole of England is about to explode.

It's 'Golden Goal' time in the semi-final of Euro '96 and all it needs is the faintest of touches to send England into the final. But Gazza has checked his run momentarily, anticipating a touch from the keeper, and as he stretches desperately for the ball it slips agonisingly past his foot and away to safety. If only Gazza hadn't cut his toenails...

Eight years on, that epic semi-final is just one of the great memories of Euro '96. It was the tournament critics said would be blighted by crowd trouble off the pitch and England's team of disgraced no-hopers on it. But in fact Euro '96 turned out to be a joyous festival of football in which the game we gave to the world really did 'come home' – even if the England team didn't manage to go all the way.

So near: Gazza comes within centimetres of putting England in the final.

With four groups of four teams, Euro '96 was the biggest European Championship ever, and all the big guns were involved. Hosts England, Germany, Holland, Italy, Spain plus shock 1992 winners Denmark, up-and-coming France and dark horses like Romania, Bulgaria, Croatia, the highly unfancied Czech Republic, and the Scots of course.

But England's campaign began inauspiciously. If Alan Shearer's international goal drought wasn't enough (he'd gone 19 months without an England goal), pictures of, ahem, high-spirited players in a nightclub during a pre-tournament tour to the Far East had the tabloids in a frenzy. Even with a Shearer goal, a stuttering 1–1 draw in the opening match against Switzerland didn't help.

But that all changed a week later when England faced the Scots at Wembley. With 76,864 fans packed inside, the famous old stadium was bathed in sunshine as England beat their arch rivals 2–0 with a slice of luck (Seaman saving McAllister's blasted penalty with his elbow) and a touch of genius (Gazza's exquisite lob and volley, followed by joyous 'dentist's chair' celebrations).

After the final whistle the English fans stayed in the stadium to sing and dance along to 'Football's Coming Home'. By the end of England's final Wembley group game against Holland, the whole nation was rocking to Skinner and Baddiel's unofficial anthem. As a *FourFourTwo* magazine reporter wrote after Terry Venables' team had given the highly-rated Holland team a lesson in total football and a 4-1 thrashing: "Just who wears the clogs in international football now?"

But it wasn't just at Wembley where the

The 'SAS' partnership between Alan Shearer and Teddy Sheringham was a key factor in England's Euro '96 run.

tournament had taken off. In Birmingham the Scots had come within a whisker of qualification. With Scotland relying on goal difference, Villa Park had even witnessed the unlikely occurrence of the Tartan Army cheering England goals as they rattled in against the Dutch. Ally McCoist's strike gave Craig Brown's men a 1–0 win against the Swiss and if Patrick Kluivert hadn't scored a late consolation at Wembley, the Scots would have made it through to the quarters.

And it was in the quarter-finals that people sat up and started to take notice of the Czechs, when Karel Poborsky sent them through to the last four with an outrageous scooped lob against Portugal. In the other matches, Germany efficiently dispatched the Croatians and their army of passionate fans, France beat the Dutch on penalties and England took the nation to the brink of a nervous breakdown. A tense and golden goalless 0–0 draw with Spain led to a penalty shoot-out in which David Seaman, with a dive to his left, and Stuart Pearce, with a 1990-demon-exorcising piledriver, were the heroes.

**"The ball slipped agonisingly past his foot and away to safety. If only Gazza hadn't cut his toenails..."**

And so it was onto the semi-finals, both of which went to penalties too (UEFA's 'Golden Goal' experiment did not appear to be working). The Czechs beat a young France team at Old Trafford (they'd be back) and then on that sultry July evening Wembley witnessed that heroic end-to-end contest between two of football's giants. Shearer, who finished the tournament's top scorer with five goals, opened the scoring only for Kuntz to equalise. In extra-time Anderton hit the post and Kuntz had a header disallowed before Gazza's toe so nearly snatched victory.

It was agony, but it got worse when, with all of the first 10 penalties converted, up stepped Gareth Southgate to scuff his way reluctantly into the history books.

England was devastated but proud. Soon-to-be Prime Minister Tony Blair described the tournament as having a "carnival atmosphere" and claimed it "demonstrated our passion for football and our capacity for friendship".

Meanwhile, Terry Venables captured the prevailing mood of the nation as he lamented: "There is nothing to be downhearted about... apart from the result!"

Germany scored football's first ever 'Golden Goal' to beat the Czechs in the final. But as Jurgen Klinsmann climbed the Wembley steps to accept the trophy from the Queen, even German fans were singing "Football's Coming Home".

## ZINEDINE ZIDANE | FRANCE

"Zidane is a player who has everything. It's impossible to take the ball from him – he is probably the best player in the world at the moment.

"The first time I heard about him was when he played in France because a friend of mine alerted me to this young midfielder he knew. I saw videos of him and I knew then he was going to be a great player.

"He just seems to have so much time on the ball... He should be free to play in the centre of midfield because if you give him the ball he will make things happen."

10

# FAN-TASTIC!

| | ITALY | FRANCE | HOLLAND | SWEDEN | GERMANY | CZECH REP | PORTUGAL |
|---|---|---|---|---|---|---|---|
| **FAVE CHANT** | **"Italia, Italia!"** … Do we really need to translate? | **"Allez Les Bleus!"** "Go the Blues!" | **"Hup Holland HUP!"** "Go, Holland, GO!" | **"Vi ar Svenska fans allihoopa"** "We are all Swedish fans" (so simple but so true!) | **"Football's Coming Home"** Well, s'pose they did win Euro '96! | **"Hosi Bojovat!"** "Come on, boys!" | **"Portugal, Portugal!"** Not too tricky to translate... and you'll be hearing it plenty this summer. |
| **FOOTIE TALK** | **Hello:** Ciao **What's the score?** Quanto stiamo? **Offside:** Fuorigioco | **Hello:** Bonjour **What's the score?** Ou en sommes nous? **Offside:** Hors jeu | **Hello:** Hallo **What's the score?** Was is der stand? **Offside:** Buitenspel | **Hello:** Hej **What's the score?** Vad stad det? **Offside:** Er, offside! | **Hello:** Guten tag **What's the score?** Wie stehts? **Offside:** Abseits | **Hello:** Ahoj **What's the score?** Jaky je? **Offside:** Mimo hru | **Hello:** Bom dia **What's the score?** Que é a contagem? **Offside:** For a de jogo |
| **MATCH GRUB** | You're joking! After all that pasta and pizza, a small, super-strong digestion-assisting coffee ('café borghetti') is all your average fan can stomach at the match. | A five-course meal with the entire family, including soup, paté, snails and cheese to finish... either that or saucissons (sausages) or frites (chips) at half-time. | The Dutch love their chips and mayonnaise, which they call 'frietsaus' (chip sauce)... well, red ketchup clashes terribly with orange! | Wrap a thin piece of bread into a cone and slap a dollop of mashed potato in. Stick a sausage in the mash and sprinkle with dried onions and you've got a 'Tunnbrodsrulle'. | Big, small, spicy, with or without mustard, the Germans love their sausages… although it brings out the Wurst in them! | The 'klobasa' is not just one of the biggest, fattest sausages in the whole of Europe, in some countries it would also be classed as an offensive weapon! | Before kick-off the streets outside Portuguese grounds turn into giant tapas bars. It's all here, from fresh grilled sardines to fried pork skin (delicious, honest), and pork steak sarnies ('Bifanas'). |
| **PRE-MATCH TIPPLE** | Coffee usually prepares the Italian fan for the emotional rollercoaster ahead. Those in need of alcoholic assistance can always add a shot of 'grappa' (rocket-fuel spirit made from grape skins) to their espresso. | Glass of vin rouge, and perhaps a small glass of beer at the ground. | Fizzy beer served in small glasses, and on special occasions the unusual flavour of the egg-based liqueur (Dick) Advocaat is popular. | Beer, beer and more beer. None of your fancy wines or cocktails Well, when you've got a viking's physique to maintain… | Absolutely enormous beers served in steins, decorative Joe Cole-sized glasses with lids (designed to disguise the fact that half of what's inside is froth!). | In the Czech Rep, home of the original Budweiser, beer is the national drink. Called Pivo, it is also cheap enough to consume in large enough quantities to keep out the cold. | Portugal is famous for its Port, but we're not talking the sweet stuff your granny drinks. This is dry, crisp and refreshing. Another local favourite is cherry brandy. |
| **DRESS CODE** | In Italy it's all about style, and Italians want to look good on the terraces. So no Roman soldier costumes or men dressed as pizza, but plenty of cool shades and well-pressed shirts. | You're more likely to see a Frenchman in a stripey shirt, beret, string of onions combo on *'Allo 'Allo* than in Portugal. The craziest you might see is an Arsenal away shirt. | Gorilla suits, santa suits, boiler suits, hats in the shape of windmills or enormous chunks of cheese and, of course, clogs... as long as it's orange anything goes with these Dutch fans. For sure. | No self-respecting Swedish footie fan would be seen dead without their viking hat. It's not just nordic pride though, the modern version (plastic) has removable horns for drinking beer out of. | Moustaches, denim jacket covered in badges, scarves tied around wrists. Well, it's either that or full lederhosen, but it's not so easy getting through customs these days wearing that garb. | Not known for their crazy costumes, the Czech supporters will probably not be the most colourful bunch at Euro 2004. | Not known for dressing up, but expect an explosion of Portuguese pride this summer. Replica shirts, scarves, caps and coloured wigs... they'll be pulling out all the stops to prove they are more colourful than Spain. |
| **CUSTOMS** | You won't see the spectacular 'tifosi' choreographed displays of flags and coloured cards common in Serie A. Spontaneous waving of arms and despairing looks to the heavens are more likely. | French fans are not as flamboyant as their team – well, when you're reigning European champions you can afford to take your football seriously. If you see a stray monsieur in a chicken suit (okay, cockerel), he's probably a confused rugby fan. | Perhaps not as crazy as their wacky outfits suggest, once the stadium is so orange it can be seen from space, they like to sit back and wait for 'total football' to triumph. | Supporters of league teams pride themselves on their Italian-style 'tifosi' displays. As football overtakes ice hockey as Sweden's number one sport, this may catch on among national team fans this summer. | German fans are organised and very vocal. Keep an eye on the crowd when they've got a corner: they'll all hold their arms out, shake their hands and cheer in crescendo until the ball is kicked. | What they lack in wackiness (even Karel Poborsky's had his hair cut!), the Czechs make up for in pride for their relatively recently formed republic. Expect plenty of red-white-and-blue flag-waving. | The Portuguese are the European 'swirling the scarf round your head' champions. It looks pretty stupid when you do it on your own at a Third Division match, but when 80,000 are at it, it's a pretty impressive sight. |

**In the spirit of goodwill, we present a light-hearted guide to help you get on with the fans of all 15 other competing nations you may meet in Portugal this summer**

| SPAIN | DENMARK | GREECE | SWITZERLAND | BULGARIA | CROATIA | LATVIA | RUSSIA |
|---|---|---|---|---|---|---|---|
| **"Espana, Espana"** "Spain, Spain". But you won't hear Catalans or Basques shouting it... | **"Og det var Danmark (x2), Olé, Olé, Olé!"** ("And it is Denmark [repeat x2], Ole, Ole, Ole!). | **"Hellas, Hellas"** "Greece, Greece" | **"Hopp Sehwiz; Allez La Suisse; or Forza Svizzera"** "Go Switzerland" for German, French or Italian Swiss. | **"Bulgari iunatsey"** "Bulgarian heroes" chanted over and over, particularly after a goal. | **"Naprijd Vatreni"** "Go Fire" ("Vatreni" is the nickname of the Croatian team). | "We will be the best, and if God will let us, we will go on for as far as we can..." And that's just the last verse! | **"Davay!"** "Go for it" ... or if things aren't going well **"Durak!"** ("idiot!"). |
| **Hello:** Hola<br>**What's the score?** Como esta o jogo?<br>**Offside:** For a de jogo | **Hello:** God dag<br>**What's the score?** Hvad er stillengen?<br>**Offside:** Offside | **Hello:** Yassas<br>**What's the score?** To abodesmata<br>**Offside:** Aristeri | **Hello:** Bonjour (Fr)<br>**What's the score?** Wie stehts? (Ger)<br>**Offside:** Fuorigioco (It) | **Hello:** Zdravei<br>**What's the score:** Kak e igra?<br>**Offside:** Zasada | **Hello:** Bok!<br>**What's the score:** Koji je rezultat?<br>**Offside:** Ofsajd | **Hello:** Sveiki<br>**What's the score?** Kads Revultats<br>**Offside:** Aizmugure | **Hello:** Zdavstvuyte<br>**What's the score?** Kak schyot?<br>**Offside:** Nye igri |
| Virtually every Spanish fan takes a ham and cheese sarnie ('bocadillo') to the match, wrapped in a white paper handkerchief. The hanky comes in useful later (see customs). | The Danes have taken the good old hot dog and made it better, with a toasted bun, a sprinkling of dried onions and a kind of cucumber relish called 'ajurkesalat'. | True Greek kebabs (or 'gyros') are a million miles from your average Saturday night large doner, and their sausages ('lukaniko') aren't bad either. | They're big on sausages in Switzerland too, and 'pommes frites' (chips) with mayonnaise. Then of course there's holey Swiss cheese! | Sunflower seeds served in cones made out of newspaper are the staple diet of Bulgarian footie fans | The Croatian burger is called a 'cevapi', and consists of a wedge of Turkish-style grilled meat stuffed into bread. | As well as the traditional Eastern European kebabs ('shaslik'), Latvian local delicacies include 'piragi' (blobs of dough with various stuffings) or 'pelmeni' (a kind of ravioli) | Grilled kebabs called 'shaslik' keep Russian fans warm at the match, and they are also rather partial to sandwiches called 'butterbroti' filled with either ham or caviar. |
| Beer, served in small glasses and known as 'canas', and red wine wash down the pre-match tapas. | There's only one drink for the Danes, and it's probably the best pre-match tipple in the world... | After a pre-match shot or two of cloudy aniseed rocket fuel 'ouzo', it's a wonder Greek fans make it to the match at all! | After a hard day's mountaineering, the Swiss recuperate with hot chocolate or 'gluwein' (sweet mulled wine) before heading off to the match. | Bulgarians love their fine home-produced wine, and it's cheap. Oh, and if you ever drink with a Bulgarian fan, always look him or her in the eye as you clink glasses. It's rude not to. | Beer, beer and more beer. After years of war and oppression, these boys are thirsty. | Since 1755, Latvians have drunk a terrifying drink called Black Balsam, a 45 per cent proof, jet black liquor, made from plants, flowers, buds, juices, roots, oils and berries! | A shot of vodka apparently does wonders for the pre-match optimism. Half a bottle and the tournament's as good as won! |
| If you see an outrageously dressed Spaniard wearing a beret and banging a drum that's Spain's most famous fan, Manolo. The rest are quite low-key, and even face painting just means a little flag on the cheek. | The Danes take a cue from the Dutch when it comes to dressing up for the football. If it's red and white great, if it's ridiculous even better. Regulation viking hats, curly wigs and Danish flag glasses will all be on view. | You'll be able to tell the Greek fans by their spectacular moustaches and the scarves tied round their heads. Rumours that some will turn up in Portugal dressed as Trojan warriors are unconfirmed. | You might get the odd cuckoo clock hat, but generally a red scarf or a replica shirt is regarded as an outlandish get-up in Switzerland. | Don't expect fancy dress (and no, not just because Uncle Bulgaria costumes are too hot for Portugal in summer). Sporting the national colours of red, green and white is as far as the Bulgarians will go. | Your average Croatia fan is a walking contradiction. i.e. a six-foot-four skinhead dressed in Auntie Betty's old tablecloth! | Until the last few months, ice hockey has always been Latvia's main sport, so what their new-found football fans will be wearing in Portugal is anyone's guess to be honest! | If the Russian fans turn up in their traditional fur hats, and big mink coats they're going to suffer in the Portuguese sunshine... |
| If the white hankies come out things are either going really well or really badly. Swirled in the air above their heads, this hanky-panky can express delight at a great goal or disgust at a shocking display. | Singing, singing and more singing. One song even goes: "That was such a wonderful song, let's sing it one more time!" | The Greeks like to let off steam at the football. That means turning up hours before the game, unfurling huge banners, jumping up and down, letting off flares and making loads of noise... until the first goal goes in against them! | Perhaps surprisingly for a country made up of German, French and Italian communities, the Swiss are not known as a football crazy nation. Swiss fans will scream for their team, but in a very polite, family-orientated way. | The Bulgarians might not travel to Portugal in their thousands, but those that make the trip will be loud and proud. | Croatian supporters are passionate alright. The fans of Hajduk Split are credited with creating the 'ultras' style copied by Italian fans. The problem is at national team games they spend half the time taunting their rivals from Dynamo Zagreb. | The Latvian supporters are known for their friendliness, and their post-match parties with opposition fans – win, lose or draw – are legendary. | As the Russian fans showed in their play-off matches with Wales, they can be vociferous without exactly being colourful. Expect mass waving of the white-red-and-blue flag if they do well. |

# ACTION MAN

**Whether he's tackling, pinging 50-yard passes or driving into the opposition's penalty box, Steven Gerrard is a vital, forceful presence in the England team...**

AS SOMEONE WHO CAME, SAW AND almost conquered, Paul Gascoigne recognises a talismanic midfielder, capable of taking his team to great heights, when he sees one. And in Steven Gerrard, he sees exactly that.

"He is different class," claims the man who inspired England in some of their finest performances of the nineties, "a truly world-class performer".

Gascoigne is hardly alone in his opinion. It's easy to forget that Steven is still only 24, such is the pace with which his reputation has grown.

"I think he's absolutely fantastic," agrees Alan Hansen. "Just watching how he's progressed in the last three or four years – we say that Wayne Rooney has everything, but so does Steven Gerrard. He's competitive, he's quick, he's brilliant on the ball. He's got the lot."

Indeed, if you were creating a blueprint for the modern footballer, it would surely come out looking something pretty close to Steven Gerrard. Brought up in various footballing academies and schools of excellence, he's one of the new breed of English player. His managers have been men like Sven-Goran Eriksson and Gérard Houllier. His team-mates and colleagues have come from all over the world. This is not an 'up and at 'em' kind of footballer. This is a skilled sportsman who's learned his trade in every position from left back to right midfield. Physically powerful but with a game based on skill rather than brawn, he has already developed into a world-class midfielder.

That development will be on display this summer in Portugal, when Gerrard will line up for his country against some of the finest players in the world. It's a challenge he's eager to meet.

"I can't wait, to be honest," he grins, fresh from an intensive session at Liverpool's Melwood training ground.

"These are the tournaments, and the matches, you watch as a kid and dream of being a part of. I remember sitting at home with my Mum and Dad and my brother when Italia '90 was on the telly, you know. I was leaping around the house when the penalties were on... you think how it would be great to be a part of that, to have the kind of imapact Paul Gascoigne did then, when he was setting the whole tournament on fire."

**"Watching Italia '90, I thought how great it would be to make the impact Gazza did."**

Like Gascoigne, Gerrard is more than capable of doing just that. He may garner less media attention than David Beckham or headline glory than Michael Owen but he is every bit as crucial to the side.

"I'm not really interested in that sort of media attention anyway, I just want to become as good a footballer as I can. I've been playing with Michael since we were kids and he was always turning heads because of how many goals he scored. And David is great to play alongside. He's a footballer anyone would want in their team, because he has such a good understanding of the game.

This relaxed attitude has stood Gerrard in good stead. Before the Turkey game, the whole Rio business, the crucial importance of the match ahead, and the subsequent shennanigans in the tunnel at half-time could have driven anyone to distraction but the midfielder took it all in his stride.

"Yes, it was a strange week in the lead-up to the Turkey game," he admits with a smile. "But we just impressed upon everyone the importance of sticking together and that showed in our performance. As for the tunnel stuff, I was looking around for a crash helmet and then I was going to go in! No, in all honesty I just waited for it to die down and then I walked through. It was just argy-bargy stuff, nothing more than that. When it calmed down I just looked around and walked through. The important thing is the team stuck together, got the right result and now we can look forward to the European Championship finals in Portugal – it will be well worth the wait after qualifying."

And how does Gerrard fancy his own chances of 'setting a tournament on fire'? After all, when he plays for England we have a habit of winning...

"Well, it's certainly not the case that if I play, England win – we have too many other talented players to suggest so much relies on me. But of course it's a good record that we've won all the games I've played in and it's one I would like to hang onto."

Here's hoping he hangs on to that record all the way to the final.

# THE KNOWLEDGE

**With another big tournament on the horizon, how much do you know about England's European Championship history? Brush up on your Euro trivia with these multiple-choice teasers...**

**1 With which band did Frank Skinner and David Baddiel record England's Euro '96 song 'Three Lions'?**

**A** Coldplay
**B** The Lightning Seeds
**C** New Order

**2 England's record win at Wembley was 9–0 against Luxembourg in a Euro qualifier in December 1982. Who scored a hat-trick that night?**

**A** Tony Woodcock
**B** Luther Blissett
**C** Glenn Hoddle

**3 Who was England's manager at the start of the Euro 2000 qualifying campaign?**

**A** Kevin Keegan
**B** Glenn Hoddle
**C** Howard Wilkinson

**4 At Euro '92, manager Graham Taylor controversially substituted Gary Lineker against Sweden in his 80th and final international appearance. Which player replaced Lineker?**

**A** Alan Smith
**B** Ian Wright
**C** Alan Shearer

**5 At which ground did England draw disappointingly with Macedonia in the second qualifier for Euro 2004, in October 2002?**

**A** Bloomfield Road, Blackpool
**B** Old Trafford, Manchester
**C** St Mary's Stadium, Southampton

**6 David Seaman saved a penalty by which player when England beat Scotland 2–0 at Wembley in Euro '96?**

**A** Gary McAllister
**B** Ally McCoist
**C** Alan Hansen

**7 Against which team were England playing when they were eliminated from Euro 2000?**

**A** Portugal
**B** Romania
**C** Germany

Question Four: Gary Lineker trudges off, but who replaced him?

**8 Which England player was sent off for apparently swearing in Italian at Italian referee Pierluigi Collina in England's opening qualifier for Euro 2000 against Sweden?**

**A** Paul Scholes
**B** Paul Gascoigne
**C** Paul Ince

**9 Which striker was England's top scorer at Euro '96 with five goals?**

**A** Alan Shearer
**B** Andy Cole
**C** Robbie Fowler

**10** How many goals did captain David Beckham score during England's Euro 2004 qualifying campaign?

**A** Five
**B** Six
**C** Two

**11** Who scored a hat-trick for England against Poland at Wembley during the qualifying campaign for Euro 2000?

**A** Paul Scholes
**B** Emile Heskey
**C** Alan Shearer

**12** Who became England's youngest-ever goal-scorer when he netted against Macedonia at the age of 17 years and 317 days?

**A** Michael Owen
**B** Joe Cole
**C** Wayne Rooney

**13** Which England player missed the final penalty that handed a semi-final shoot-out victory to Germany at Euro '96?

**A** Gareth Southgate
**B** Tony Adams
**C** Paul Ince

**14** In their eight Euro 2004 qualifiers, how many times did England come back from a 1–0 half-time deficit to win 2–1?

**A** One
**B** Three
**C** Five

**15** Who are the only two players to have been sent off while representing England on home soil, both in European Championship qualifiers?

**A** Paul Scholes and Alan Smith
**B** Paul Ince and David Beckham
**C** David Batty and Ray Wilkins

**16** Who scored all five goals in England's 5–0 European Championship qualifier thrashing of Cyprus in April 1975, thus equalling the record number of goals in a game by an England player?

**A** Mick Channon
**B** Kevin Keegan
**C** Malcolm Macdonald

**17** Who scored England's second goal against Portugal in the opening match of the 2000 finals?

**A** Steve McManaman
**B** Paul Scholes
**C** Sol Campbell

**18** Only two managers have taken England to the semi-finals of the European Championships. Who were they?

**A** Sir Alf Ramsey and Terry Venables
**B** Glenn Hoddle and Kevin Keegan
**C** Terry Venables and Ron Greenwood

**19** Which England players became known as 'SAS' for their explosive partnership at Euro '96?

**A** Paul Scholes and Teddy Sheringham
**B** Alan Shearer and Stuart Pearce
**C** Alan Shearer and Teddy Sheringham

**20** England have never won the European Championship. But which of our rivals holds the record number of tournament wins with three?

**A** Germany
**B** France
**C** Holland

## ANSWERS

**1**. B. The Lightning Seeds
**2**. B. Luther Blissett
**3**. B. Glenn Hoddle
**4**. A. Alan Smith (the former Arsenal striker)
**5**. C. St Mary's Stadium, Southampton
**6**. A. Gary McAllister
**7**. B. Romania
**8**. C. Paul Ince
**9**. A. Alan Shearer
**10**. A. Five
**11**. A. Paul Scholes
**12**. C. Wayne Rooney
**13**. A. Gareth Southgate
**14**. B. Three
**15**. A. Paul Scholes and Alan Smith (Scholes against Sweden, 5 June 1999; Smith (the Leeds United striker) against Macedonia, 16 October 2002)
**16**. C. Malcolm Macdonald
**17**. A. Steve McManaman
**18**. A. Sir Alf Ramsey and Terry Venables (in 1968 and 1996)
**19**. C. Alan Shearer and Teddy Sheringham
**20**. A. Germany

# THE POWER BEHIND SVEN

It takes more than one man to cater for the diverse needs of an international football squad. Fortunately, Sven has a strong coaching team offering support...

TORD GRIP

SVEN'S RIGHT-HAND MAN, Tord Grip joined the England set-up in winter 2000. His first match as part of the staff was against Spain at Villa Park in February 2001. Coincidentally, back in 1961, the Swede joined Aston Villa on a three-month loan from from Swedish first division club Degerfors.

Later, he played for AIK in Stockholm and earned three caps for Sweden.

A spell as player/manager of KB Karlskoga was followed by managerial stints at Örebro and Degerfors which led to the job of coaching the Swedish women's team and then the men's U-16 and U-21 sides. Tord also coached the full Norwegian team but has now settled into a comfortable working partnership with Sven. The two have worked together with the Swedish national team, and in Serie A at Lazio, before linking up again for England. Both men share a belief in team spirit and simple management.

"We have some very talented individuals," says Tord, "but if everyone plays together as a team, we can achieve almost anything."

BRIAN KIDD

THE FORMER MANCHESTER United and Leeds first-team coach joined Sven's team in January 2003. Sven declared: "Brian is a very good coach and already has international experience. Plus, he knows more than half of the squad players and is very popular with them."

A Manchester United fan born and bred, Kiddo joined the club as a schoolboy and celebrated his 19th birthday by scoring in United's 4–1 extra-time triumph over Benfica in the 1968 European Cup final.

He also played for Arsenal, Manchester City, Everton and Bolton in a distinguished career.

Brian's first managerial post was at Barrow and then he had a couple of number two jobs at Swindon and Preston. He had been Preston manager for three months, when Alex Ferguson brought him to United as director of the School of Excellence. He went on to become Fergie's assistant and in 1993 helped United to their first League title in 26 years. After years of success, he moved to Blackburn and then on to Leeds before getting the call from Sven.

SAMMY LEE

SCOUSER SAMMY PLAYED FOR Liverpool for 11 years and was a fans' favourite for his boyish enthusiasm for the game – a quality he still retains as an England coach.

In his playing career, he won two European Cups, three League Championships and four League Cups. He also played for England 14 times, scoring twice. After Liverpool, he had spells with QPR and Osasuna in Spain.

Graeme Souness appointed him reserve team coach at Liverpool and he became first-team coach before joining the England set-up.

RAY CLEMENCE

IN A GLITTERING CAREER, THE former Liverpool and England goalkeeper won three European Cups, two UEFA Cups, five League Championships, one FA Cup and one League Cup. He also won 61 England caps, a number that would have been even higher if Peter Shilton hadn't also been competing for the keeper's jersey.

Ray went on to play for Spurs, reaching a further two FA Cup finals. He managed Barnet before Glenn Hoddle entrusted him with the job of England goalkeeping coach in 1996.

DAVE SEXTON

73-YEAR-OLD DAVE IS ONE OF the most admired coaches in the game. A former player, he got his first managerial role at Leyton Orient in 1965. He went on to manage many of Britain's biggest clubs, including Chelsea, QPR and Manchester United.

The England U-21 team won the UEFA Championship twice under his command and The FA were so impressed they made him the first technical director of the FA National School at Lilleshall in 1984. He remains an integral part of the England set-up.

## PAVEL NEDVED | CZECH REPUBLIC

"I know Pavel very well because I had him at Lazio for three-and-a-half years and at that time he played in left midfield.

"He is a very complete football player as he is hard working, skilful and technically very competent. He can use both his left and his right foot for everything – he can cross with both, he can shoot with both and he can pass with both.

"He is also a match winner because he scores so many goals."

# MOORO
## THE GREATEST OF THEM ALL

**When asked to name the best England player of the last 50 years, half of the nation's football fans voted for the legendary Bobby Moore. Let us pay tribute to the only England captain ever to lift a major championship trophy...**

BOBBY MOORE PLAYED FOR ENGLAND 108 times, captained the team in 90 matches (a record he holds jointly with Billy Wright) and famously led the Three Lions to 1966 World Cup glory.

Born Robert Frederick Chelsea Moore in Barking on 12 April 1941, he grew up to play for his beloved West Ham United, making his debut against Manchester United on 8 September 1958. He would go on to play in the claret and blue for 15 years making 544 League appearances and scoring 24 goals. In the 1963/64 season, he helped the Hammers to win The FA Cup and was also named Footballer of the Year and a year later added a European Cup-Winners' Cup medal to his trophy cabinet.

By the time Sir Alf Ramsey took over as England manager in 1963, Bobby was already captain and this arrangement suited the new boss perfectly. The fact that Bobby went on to win exactly 100 of his international caps playing under Ramsey demonstrates how much faith the legendary manager had in him.

On 30 July 1966, Bobby enjoyed his finest hour, leading England's 'wingless wonders' to a famous 4–2 extra-time victory over West Germany in the World Cup Final at Wembley. The iconic image of Bobby holding the Jules Rimet trophy aloft is engrained on every England fan's memory, sustaining us through many disappointments in the 38 years since.

Two years later, he led the England side to third place in the 1968 European Championship, (a feat not equalled by an England team until Euro '96) before attempting to retain the World Cup at Mexico '70. A heartbreaking 3–2 defeat by West Germany denied England at the quarter-final stage, but Bobby's performance in a group match against eventual winners Brazil, where he made one brilliant tackle after another, was one of the finest-ever by an England player.

On 14 November 1973, aged 32, he made his 108th and final appearance for England in a 0–1 defeat by Italy. He continued to show his class at domestic level though. In 1974, he joined Fulham and went on to make another 124 League appearances for the Cottagers. He also enjoyed one more FA Cup Final date in 1975, ironically against his old club West Ham who prevailed by a 2–0 scoreline.

In 1991, Bobby was diagnosed with cancer and he died two years later on 24 February 1993 aged just 51. English football had prematurely lost not just it's greatest-ever player but also one of the nicest people ever to play the game.

### ENGLAND'S GREATEST PLAYER

**1953–2003: THE TOP 10**

Mooro polled a whopping 50 per cent of the vote, and his nearest challenger Nat Lofthouse was second on 18 per cent. In third place was Sir Bobby Charlton with 10 per cent. Here's the top 10 in full...

**1 BOBBY MOORE 1962–1973**
England's World Cup-winning captain also led the team to third place in the 1968 European Championship.

**2 NAT LOFTHOUSE 1950–58**
The 'Lion of Vienna' scored twice in a match on 12 occasions, plundering 30 goals in 33 England appearnces.

**3 SIR BOBBY CHARLTON 1958–70**
1966 World Cup hero Sir Bobby scored more goals for the Three Lions than any other player, striking 49 times in 106 appearances.

**4 DAVID BECKHAM 1996–**
David has proved his class and character by coming back from the controversy of World Cup '98 to become England's inspirational captain.

**5 SIR STANLEY MATTHEWS 1934–57**
The 'Wizard Of The Dribble', winger Stanley scored 11 goals in 54 England games in an international career spanning over 22 years.

**6 ALAN SHEARER 1992–2000**
Alan was top scorer at Euro '96 with five goals and his 30-goal career total puts him joint fourth on the all-time England goalscorers' list.

**7 GARY LINEKER 1984–92**
Finished one short of Sir Bobby Charlton's 49-goal career haul, but Gary scored more goals (10) in the World Cup finals than any other England player.

**8 PAUL GASCOIGNE 1988–1998**
Famously described by Sir Bobby Robson as "daft as a brush", but Gazza's sublime skills thrilled England fans at Italia '90 and Euro '96.

**9 JIMMY GREAVES 1959–67**
One of the most natural finishers ever to play the game, Greavsie scored 44 goals (including six hat-tricks) in a 57-match international career.

**10 KEVIN KEEGAN 1972-82**
The striker (and future England boss) was twice voted European Footballer Of The Year and is the highest-placed player from the 1970s.

# PACESETTER

**Wayne Rooney has hit the top in record time. Everyone from Alan Shearer to Ronaldo is queuing up to proclaim him as the next big thing, but 'Roonaldo' himself is just happy to be part of the team...**

A FEVER IS ABOUT TO HIT PORTUGAL, and its roots can be traced to the Saturday in October 2002 when 16-year-old Wayne Rooney deftly controlled an up-and-under from Thomas Gravesen and curled a wickedly powerful shot into the top corner of David Seaman's net.

That goal not only made Rooney the Premiership's youngest goalscorer, it sparked 'Rooneymania' as an entire nation finally cottoned on to the extent of the talent Evertonians had been jealously guarding.

"Remember the name," cried commentator Clive Tyldesley as the youngster was mobbed by his Everton team-mates, "Wayne Rooney!"

But nobody was ever likely to forget, least of all an awe-struck Arsene Wenger.

"This lad is the complete footballer at 16," marvelled the Arsenal boss after seeing his team's 30-match unbeaten run shattered. "I have never seen better at his age."

"Rooney's something special," proclaimed Alan Shearer. "This boy is our next world-class player," chipped in Paul Gascoigne. Even Ronaldo got in on the act. "From what I've seen," said the Real Madrid superstar, "this boy has both a big present and a big future."

Talk about pressure. Overnight Rooney became a household name. "People see me in the streets who would never have known who I was before so I get asked for a lot of autographs," says Wayne, now 18, as we sit in a Manchester photographic studio, contemplating the way his life changed. "It's good. It shows I'm getting somewhere."

If Rooney felt the pressure brought on by his sudden fame, he certainly never showed it. So impressive was he in the months after *that* goal that Sven-Goran Eriksson could not resist calling him up to his squad for the friendly with Australia in February despite having seen him play live for only 25 minutes.

"I was in the treatment room, messing around with a few of the lads and the manager [David Moyes] came in and told me I was in the England squad," Wayne recalls. "I thought he meant the Under-21s. When I realised it was the full squad, I was shocked."

Shocked, perhaps. Overawed, never.

Rooney became England's youngest ever player, but it was the way he fitted into the senior squad that impressed older colleagues.

**"It was brilliant to qualify for Euro 2004 because we'd worked so hard. It was a real team effort."**

"When you first join up with England, you can be training with players you supported as a child, but he wasn't starry-eyed," said Rio Ferdinand. "He just seemed confident."

A late substitute appearance against Liechtenstein set the scene for a starring role in the crunch Group Seven match at home to Turkey in April. With England needing to win, Rooney turned in a scintillating performance, brimming with strength, aggression and skill, that lifted the crowd and inspired his team-mates to a 2–0 victory.

"We weren't the best in the first 10 minutes, but once the game settled down, I got into the game more and more," says Wayne. "For a while, I thought we weren't going to score, but Darius Vassell came off the bench and got the first and after that, we were confident we'd win."

England had a new saviour. one-nil down in Macedonia and staring disaster in the face, it was Rooney who struck the crucial equaliser, steering in Emile Heskey's knock-down to take Michael Owen's record as England's youngest goalscorer.

"The keeper should have saved it," smiles Wayne, "but I was just happy to pull a goal back because we needed to score early in the second half."

England won 2–1 and, four days later, Rooney scored again as Liechtenstein were dispatched to set up the biggest game of the youngster's career: against Turkey in the pressure-cooker atmosphere of Istanbul's Sükrü Saraçoglu Stadium with a place at Euro 2004 at stake.

"The crowd was so loud you couldn't hear your team-mates shouting!" recalls Wayne. "But after 10 minutes of the warm-up you got used to it."

His eyes light up as he recalls the game's triumphant outcome.

"It was brilliant because we'd worked so hard. It was a real team effort. You could see how much it meant to all of us at the end."

What it means for Wayne now is the chance to take his skills to a truly international stage.

"Hopefully we can win the Euros," he says. "On a personal level though, I just want to stay in the team. I'm just happy to be playing for England."

Europe's defenders may not feel quite the same way.

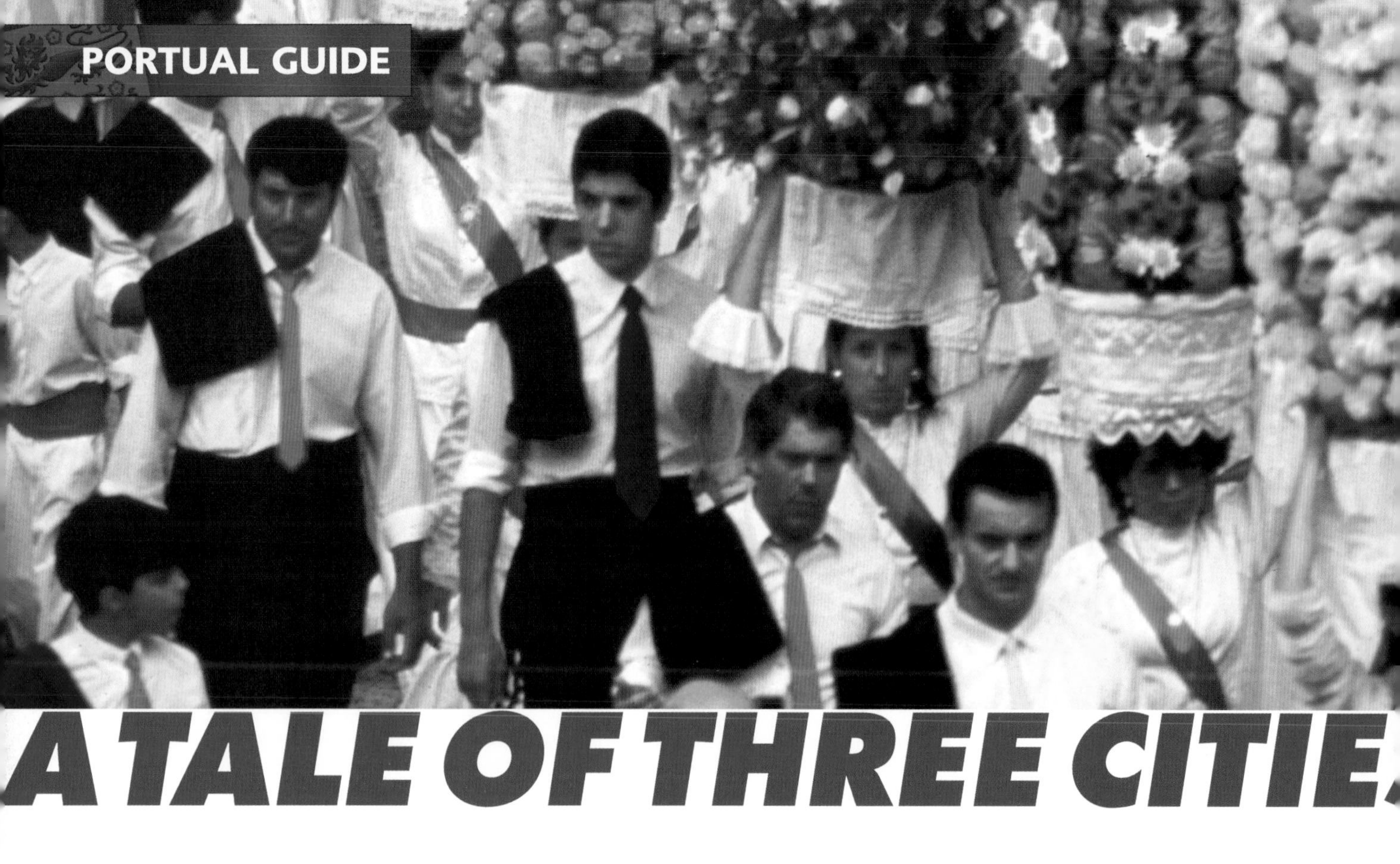

# A TALE OF THREE CITIE

**Planning to travel to the games? Then let us be your guide to the history, culture and, yes, bars, of the three cities where Sven's side may find themselves playing in Portugal...**

## LISBON

ENGLAND'S FIRST PORT OF CALL IS LISBON, where they face France at Da Luz stadium. We return to the ground for our third game, against Croatia, and – should the lads go all the way – could also find ourselves in the city for the quarters, semis and final!

One of Europe's most ancient cities, Lisbon is lively and cosmopolitan. Located on the west edge of the Iberian peninsula, almost halfway between the north and south of the country, Lisbon is the focal point of Portugal.

Although temperatures can reach 30°C in summer, an almost permanent breeze in Estoril tempers the heat. According to legend, Greek hero Ulysses founded Lisbon (it's original name was Olissipo) because of the warm climate and later on it became home to many Romans who developed it into an international city. It was the starting point of the Portuguese voyages of discovery of the 15th and 16th centuries and became a major trading centre.

Even now, culture and heritage abound throughout its narrow streets and traditional districts from the Belém riverside to the Parque das Naçoes area. The Belém district, with its monuments like the Belém tower, the Jerónimos monastery and the planetarium, is a particular favourite for tourists.

In 1755, an earthquake devastated the most densely populated areas but the reconstructed city that exists to this day centres around two big public squares – Rossio and Praça do Comércio. The old royal palace gave way to a new one at the Praça do Comércio and most government ministries are still there now. The triumphal arch over Rua Augusta, the statue of King José I and the archways that surround the square are worth seeing.

The 1940s witnessed the completion of the 25 de Abril bridge, Europe's largest suspension bridge. Another bridge was built in the 1990s, over the Tagus, and named after the country's best known navigator, Vasco da Gama.

The riverfront district 'Baixa pombalina' has a historic feel and the medieval Alfama and Mouraria neighbourhoods on the way to the capital's most ancient monument, the Sao Jorge castle, are often full of the sound of street traders loudly selling their wares.

At night, 'Fado', the traditional song heard only in Lisbon, takes over the city, especially the Bairro Alto. There, you'll find fado houses, restaurants, bars and discos known for their underground and dance music. Officially, these venues are open until 2am, but there always tends to be a party somewhere that will go on until dawn.

Since Expo '98, the newly-developed riverside areas have also become a mecca for the young once darkness falls and the bars on the Avenida 24 de Julho, Docas District and the Parque das Naçoes are often pounding to Brazilian and African beats, reflecting Lisbon's multicultural heritage.

If you're not nursing a hangover, and you've seen the sights, Lisbon has plenty else on offer. There's everything from bullfights to 'revistas' (satirical plays), contemporary ballet, art exhibitions, museums and concerts. If that sounds a little highbrow, the city also offers plenty of shopping opportunities, or you can take it easy with some sailing. The windy shores of the north provide Europe's

best waves for bodyboarding, surfing and windsurfing. The southern beaches are best for those with more leisurely pursuits in mind.

Golf lovers should have few problems as Lisbon has some dozen courses to play, around half of which are located in the holiday resorts of Estoril and Cascais.

Finally, if you're feeling lucky, you could try out Europe's biggest casino, in Estoril.

**GETTING TO THE GAMES**

Lisbon has two stadiums. The Luz Stadium (where England play France and Croatia) is situated in the northern part of Lisbon and is pretty well integrated into the city's road system. The traffic pre- and post-match flows quite well. There are also two rail stations within 2.5 kilometres of the ground, which are part of the regional and national rail and underground networks.

The José Alvalade stadium (where England could play a quarter and/or semi-final) in the north of the city is again well served by the local transport system, and can cope with a large flow of traffic before and after matches. The stadium is also served by Lisbon's underground system, which may be your best bet for getting to and from the match.

**COIMBRA**

BETWEEN THE TWO LISBON-BASED MATCHES, England travel to Coimbra, the main city of the central Beira Litoral region. Coimbra is considered the Oxford of Portugal as its university was founded in 1290 and for many years was the only one in the country.

**"Officially, bars in the Bairro Alto district of Lisbon open until 2am, but there always seems to be a party that goes on until dawn."**

Before then, Coimbra was also the capital of the Portuguese nation, built on the north bank of the Mondego river which bisects the city. The first Portuguese parliament of 1211 was established at Coimbra before Lisbon became the capital later that same century.

The city retains its sense of history. The old town centre fanning out from the university comprises narrow alleyways, lined with taverns, cafés, galleries and bookstores. Churches, cathedrals and convents of historic importance are scattered around. It is at its liveliest in May, when the end of term is celebrated with the 'Queima das Fitas', a series of concerts and performances enjoyed by the country's most prestigious students.

The town is 'guarded' by the gothic Arco de Almedina cut into the old city walls. Under the arch, past the antique shops, you reach the Se Velha, the old cathedral, a mix of Romanesque, Gothic and Renaissance styles originally begun in 1162.

Just behind it is the Velha Universidade, the main university, and the Biblioteca Geral da Universidade library. The main attractions for visitors here are the Sala dos Capelos, where graduation ceremonies are held, and the University Chapel, with tiles, a portal and a candelabra from the Ages of Discovery.

The university library is full of rare, ancient volumes, although most are not on display to the public, but the baroque decoration is still worth seeing.

The other two major attractions in town are the Museu Machado de Castro, named after a famous Portuguese sculptor, and containing ecclesiastical relics; and the Igreja e Mosteiro da Santa Cruz, a monastery founded during the reign of the first Portuguese king, Afonso Henriques, with its impressive pulpit and Manueline cloisters.

The city is not all academia and artefacts though. It also has one of the nation's biggest kids' attractions, at the Portugal dos Pequenitos, a miniature representation of famous buildings and typical farmhouses across the country.

A bus trip away is the town of Luso which is famed for its healing spas. And an hour's train journey west is Figueira da Foz, a lively resort lined with lovely beaches which attracts a lot of surfers. To the east of Coimbra, by the Spanish border, is Beiras, home of the highest mountains in Portugal, and perfect hiking country.

**GETTING TO THE GAME**

The A1/IP1 highway that links Porto and Lisbon runs close to the city, so Coimbra is easy to access from all points of Portugal, and the Coimbra City stadium has a spacious underground car park. The main express train terminus at Coimbra B station is close by, with a regular train link to Coimbra A in town. Special buses on match days are expected to run frequently before and after matches in town.

## PORTO

WHETHER OR NOT ENGLAND WILL BE travelling to Porto depends on us winning Group B and then winning our quarter-final match. If Sven's men go that route, they will travel to the city known as "the Powerhouse of the Portuguese north".

Porto is set at the mouth of the river Douro, and has two sides. On the south bank are the famous port wine lodges and on the north bank the hilly, atmospheric old quarter. Each side is linked by five vast bridges, the most spectacular being the two-level Ponte de Dom Luis I, which was built in the 19th century.

Slightly to the north is the landmark Torre dos Clérigos, which offers breathtaking views over both the whole city and the Douro estuary spreading out towards the Atlantic.

The main centre for bars and restaurants is clustered towards the waterfront, amid alleyways leading down to the old quays, Cais da Ribeira. Further south are the nearby resorts and windswept beaches of Espinho and Cortegaça.

Exposed to the Atlantic, Porto has a much wetter climate than the rest of Portugal, with lower, bearable temperatures in summer. The city also has something of a British connection, dating back to the 17th and 18th centuries when a profitable port wine trade created strong trading links with the UK (evidenced, for instance, by the old red phone boxes scattered around the city).

Starting on the Ribeira, you'll find plenty of tiny, tucked away watering holes, particularly along Rua Fonte Taurina and Rua Cimo do Muro da Ribeira. For late bars, Rua da São João will provide plenty of options.

Culture-seekers should head for the ornate Sé (Cathedral) on the north side. Nearby the Torre dos Clérigos is a baroque masterpiece, and a climb up its 240 steps will afford you the best view of the city.

**GETTING TO THE GAME**

If England play a semi-final in Porto, it will be at the Dragão Stadium. On match day, there will be special STCP buses running from the Rotunda da Boavista (Praça Mouzinho de Albuquerque) or Praça da Liberdade, all the way to the ground. Also, regular buses 21 and 78 run from the Rotunda or Avenida dos Aliados. Taxis from the centre of town are easy to find and it should cost you no more than 10 Euros to get to the ground.

### ACCOMMODATION

According to local law, accommodation in Portugal is divided into the following categories: hotel, private guest house, motel, pousada, aparthotel, quality inn, tourist apartment, tourist village, rural hotel and boarding house, and each category has its own criteria regarding stars, standards and facilities on offer.

For Euro 2004, there is an official accommodation agency to help fans:

**Euro 2004 Accommodation Agency**
**Av. Marques de Tomar, 44 - 3°**
**1050-156 Lisboa**
**Portugal**
**Tel: +351 217 615 520**
**Fax: +351 217 950 339**
**Email: accommodation.agency@aa.euro2004.pt**

The agency aims to cover all needs including accommodation and transportation and is divided into separate operations departments, namely corporate business, media, teams, supporters and transportation.

### FOOD AND DRINK

Portuguese food is mostly simple but excellent. Served in large portions it gives very good value for money. It's pretty easy to find traditional and international cuisine almost everywhere. Typical meals are:

**Breakfast**
Tends to be small and simple: bread, rolls and toast, with butter and jam, plus a coffee on the side.

**Dinner**
Often begins with soups, such as 'Caldo verde' (thick potato, cabbage and sausage soup), 'Sopa a Portuguesa' (similar to caldo verde, with the addition of beans, broccoli, carrots and turnips) or 'Conja de galinha' (chicken and rice soup). The main course usually consists of meat or fish dishes such as 'Ameijoas ne cataplano' (steamed clams, sausages, ham, white wine, tomato, onion and herbs), 'Bacalhaou' (dried salted cod, baked with parsley, potatoes, onions and olives) or 'frango' or 'galinha' – (chicken fried, grilled, barbecued, stewed or roasted).

**Desserts**
Favourites include 'pudim flan' (caramel custard) and 'arroz doce' (rice pudding and cinnamon).

**Drinks**
Portuguese wine is excellent, whether it is 'tinto' (red), 'branco' (white) or 'vinho verde' (green wine). Other common drinks are ports and Madeiras.

### LOCAL SHOPPING

Generally, shopping hours are 9am–1pm and 3pm–7pm Monday to Friday, 9am–1pm on Saturdays.

The most famous Portuguese handicrafts include 'azulejos' (painted ceramic tiles), pottery, rugs, embroidery, lace work, and wicker work. Different varieties of ceramic work are produced all over the country, using decorated, glazed or just simple brown clay. Many of the regional crafts are sold in other parts of the country, particularly Lisbon. Other shopping items include leather goods, copper, handcrafted silver and gold, tapestry, woodcarving, cork products, porcelain and china, crystal and glassware.

# THE VENUES

## THE STADIA

| CITY | STADIUM | CAPACITY |
|---|---|---|
| AVEIRO | AVEIRO MUNICIPAL | 30,000 |
| BRAGA | BRAGA MUNICIPAL | 30,000 |
| COIMBRA | COIMBRA CITY | 30,000 |
| FARO-LOULÉ | ALGARVE | 30,000 |
| GUIMARÃES | D. AFONSO HENRIQUES | 30,000 |
| LEIRIA | DR. MAGALHÃES PESSOA | 30,000 |
| LISBON | JOSÉ ALVALADE | 52,000 |
| | LUZ | 65,000 |
| PORTO | DRAGÃO | 52,000 |
| | BESSA | 30,000 |

LUZ STADIUM

COIMBRA CITY

AVEIRO MUNICIPAL STADIUM

DRAGÃO STADIUM

# THE BOSS

**Sven-Göran Eriksson leads England to his second major tournament as an England manager confident of success but with no illusions about the size of the task ahead...**

13 NOVEMBER 2003: I'M SITTING with Sven-Göran Eriksson in the sweeping reception of the Lowry Hotel in Manchester. To find two seats to perch on is something of an achievement, so sparsely furnished is the ground floor of Manchester's first-ever five-star hotel. But, dressed in a tailored charcoal suit and the epitome of calm, the England boss looks perfectly at ease in such uncluttered surroundings. England are in town to play Denmark in the first friendly match since qualifying for Euro 2004, and it's the perfect time to reflect on the campaign. Naturally, the first topic of conversation is that crucial 0–0 draw in England's final match against Istanbul.

"I was very proud of the players that night," he smiles. "We are a young team, but we played like a team with lots of experience: keeping the ball when it was right to and sometimes playing balls into the channels behind Turkey's full-backs to take pressure off the defence.

"It was a marvellous performance. I didn't care that we didn't win, even though we didn't play for a draw. I think we had the better chances and deserved to score, but the result ensured our qualification and that was the main thing. The European Championship is are almost as big a tournament as the World Cup, and we're very proud to be there again."

The draw against Turkey preserved Sven's remarkable 14-match unbeaten record in tournament qualifiers stretching back to his first competitive game as England boss, a 2–1 World Cup qualifying win over Finland in March 2001.

"The key to that is the players are not only very good, they are also very focused when there is a real game," he explains. "Our performances in friendlies haven't always been that good, but when it comes to qualifiers we have proved to be very hard to beat."

On 30 November 2003, a few weeks after our initial chat, the draw is made in Lisbon and England are pitted against France, Switzerland and Croatia. To come up against defending champions and tournament favourites France so early in the competition will be a tough test, but after the draw Sven is also quick to emphasise the dangers posed by all three teams in Group B.

**"The most important thing to me is that all of the players are fit. That is far more important to me than the draw."**

"France are the big favourites to win the tournament and that game will be very tough of course," he admits. "Croatia are technically very solid, physically strong and are very good at keeping hold of the ball. Their passing game is often frustrating because they can keep the ball for so long!

"Swiss football is progressing very quickly. They play a very mixed style of football, maybe because of their geography – in many ways they are quite German in their style but also show similarities with the Italian game. They won their qualifying group ahead of Russia and the Irish so we'll have to watch them."

Sven credits a strong teamworking ethic as the key to our own qualification success, but when pressed to talk about one particular headline-maker during the campaign, he can't hide his admiration.

"Yes, Wayne Rooney is one of the biggest talents I've ever had," he says. "He can play up front on his own or deeper where he can play other people in, dribble or take a shot.

"He doesn't seem to have any fear to go out and play. Whether it's a local game or an international match, I don't think it matters to him. He seems to be very strong mentally.

"Off the field, he is quiet so I can't say I know him very well, but he has a nice smile and always seems to be happy. He's fitted into the group very well."

Alongside the likes of Ashley Cole, Matthew Upson and Kieron Dyer, Rooney is typical of the emerging young talent being given the chance to flourish with Sven's England, but the boss is keen to pay tribute to the (relatively!) old guard too.

"Take Sol Campbell, the most experienced central defender we've got. He's a very strong, assured player and we always feel more calm when he's in there. Then we have David Beckham. He has become a great captain for us and is very influential on the younger players by the professionalism he shows on and off the pitch."

This blend of youth and experience is the cornerstone of England's Euro 2004 ambitions.

"The most important thing to me is that all of the players are fit," concludes Sven. "That is far more important to me than the draw. If they are fit, I'm confident we will have a good tournament."

## Luis Figo | Portugal

"A fantastic player – he can cross, dribble and score goals and is one of the best players in the world. His ability to hold onto the ball makes him a very useful player, but his creativity is remarkable – he makes so much happen for the players around him.

"I first heard about him when he was playing in Portuagl [for Sporting Lisbon], but it was only when he went to Barcelona that he started to show how good he is.

"He scores for Real Madrid, but he scores even more for Portugal... but maybe because Real have a certain Ronaldo and Raul in the side!"

# THE LIKELY LADS

**Sven-Goran Eriksson faces tough choices when it comes to whittling down his squad to just 23 names. Let's take a closer look at the stars hoping to make it into England's Euro 2004 party...**

## GOALKEEPERS

### DAVID JAMES

CLUB MANCHESTER CITY
BORN 1 AUGUST 1970
HEIGHT 6FT 5IN
WEIGHT 14ST 2LB
CAPS 21 (INC. 6 SUB)
GOALS CONCEDED 12

West Ham's strong, agile keeper has finally established himself as England's number one and successor to David Seaman. Long considered to be an outstanding natural talent, David is now finding the consistency required at the international level despite playing this season in the First Division. The former Liverpool goalkeeper won his first senior England cap in 1997 but has only recently become a fixture in the team. A keen student of sports psychology, he has cut down on the unforced errors that used to blight his game. David repaid Sven-Goran Eriksson's faith with a string of fine performances – most notably in the home victory over Turkey – on the road to Portugal 2004.

### PAUL ROBINSON

CLUB LEEDS UNITED
BORN 15 OCTOBER 1979
HEIGHT 6FT 4IN
WEIGHT 15ST 7LB
CAPS 4 (INC. 4 SUB)
GOALS CONCEDED 2

Paul is a surprisingly nimble keeper considering his imposing size and has the talent to become a top-class international performer. The Beverley-born custodian made his Premiership debut before his 20th birthday. And he proved he has the cool temperament required at the highest level when replacing the injured Nigel Martyn during Leeds United's rollercoaster ride to the Champions League semi-finals in 2001. Thus far, his England experience has been limited to substitute appearances in friendlies, but a bright international future seems assured.

### IAN WALKER

CLUB LEICESTER CITY
BORN 31 OCTOBER 1971
HEIGHT 6FT 2IN
WEIGHT 13ST 5LB
CAPS 3 (INC. 2 SUB)
GOALS CONCEDED 1

It is to the Leicester City goalkeeper's lasting credit that he is in the frame for Euro 2004. Ian has made only one full appearance for England, way back in February 1997. Injuries to other goalkeepers saw coach Glenn Hoddle select Ian for the crucial World Cup qualifier against Italy at Wembley. It was a baptism of fire for the then Tottenham Hotspur player, who conceded the only goal of the game to Gianfranco Zola's brilliant near-post thunderbolt. After losing his place to Neil Sullivan at Spurs, Ian has resurrected his career (appropriately) at the Walkers Stadium. Recalled by Sven in August, he will be desperate to stake his claim as one of the three keepers to go to Portugal.

## DEFENDERS

### WAYNE BRIDGE

CLUB CHELSEA
BORN 5 AUGUST 1980
HEIGHT 5FT 10IN
WEIGHT 12ST 5LB
CAPS 15 (INC. 7 SUB)
GOALS 0

Blessed with maturity and consistency beyond his years, Wayne can look forward to a second international tournament before his 24th birthday. The Chelsea defender has proved himself to be a very reliable performer and continues to mature quickly under the expert tutelage of Sven-Goran Eriksson and his club manager Claudio Ranieri. Bridge's versatility – he can operate on the left of midfield, ahead of Ashley Cole – is another reason why he looks a certainty to board the plane to Portugal in the summer.

### SOL CAMPBELL

CLUB ARSENAL
BORN 18 SEPTEMBER 1974
HEIGHT 6FT 2IN
WEIGHT 14ST 2LB
CAPS 56 (INC. 3 SUB)
GOALS 1

It has become a matter of fact that England are simply not the same team without Sol's colossal influence in the heart of defence. As Sven himself says, "We always feel more calm when he's in there." Strange to think now that he made an indifferent start to the Euro 2004 qualifying campaign when England drew with Macedonia in October 2002. He has since forged a reputation as England's Mr Reliable and defensive linchpin. The Arsenal centre-half was at his strongest and most courageous during the explosive encounter with Turkey in Istanbul that saw England qualify for Portugal 2004. Similar barnstorming performances are required this summer.

### GARETH SOUTHGATE

CLUB MIDDLESBROUGH
BORN 3 SEPTEMBER 1970
HEIGHT 5FT 10IN
WEIGHT 12ST 3LB
CAPS 55 (INC. 12 SUB)
GOALS 2

Gareth has long been a dependable part of the England defence. Seeing him play now, it is hard to believe that he was a key part of the great England team of Euro '96, because he still has such a commanding presence at the back. The intervening years have only improved the Watford-born defender whose domestic career started with Crystal Palace. He's moved further north in both his transfers, and has ended up at the heart of a tight Middlesbrough defence. He made his international debut against Portugal in 1996 and Euro 2004 would be Gareth's fourth major tournament should Sven give him the nod.

### ASHLEY COLE

CLUB ARSENAL
BORN 20 DECEMBER 1980
HEIGHT 5FT 8IN
WEIGHT 10ST 10LB
CAPS 23
GOALS 0

Since his debut against Albania at the tender age of 21, Ashley has made the left-back spot his own. Aggressive, determined and ultra-competitive, the Arsenal defender is blessed with the pace to make dangerous forays into opposition territory. That turn of speed also allows him to make up for any occasional defensive lapses that may betray his relative inexperience. It is a testament to Sven-Goran Eriksson's faith in Ashley that he has never played as a substitute for his country. Already tasting Champions League action with Arsenal, Portugal 2004 should afford him the opportunity to confirm he is one of Europe's foremost full-backs.

### JONATHAN WOODGATE

CLUB NEWCASTLE UNITED
BORN 22 JANUARY 1980
HEIGHT 6FT 2IN
WEIGHT 12ST 6LB
CAPS 4 (INC. 1 SUB)
GOALS 0

Undoubtedly a talented defender, Jonathan's progress has been hampered by injury and off-field events since his debut against Bulgaria in June 1999. The Newcastle United player will be just 24 when the European Championship begins, so time is on his side if he is to make a long-term impact at international level. But the former Leeds United centre-half has failed to appear for England in a competitive match since the disappointing 2–2 draw at home to Macedonia in October 2002. This suggests he will struggle to make the final squad this summer, but with his ability Jonathan is very capable of mounting a late bid for inclusion.

## JOHN TERRY

CLUB CHELSEA
BORN 7 DECEMBER 1980
HEIGHT 6FT 1IN
WEIGHT 12ST 13LB
CAPS 6
GOALS 0

The year 2003 was a good one for John Terry. This gritty Chelsea defender was able to transfer his consistent club form to the international stage with a series of solid displays for England. Pick of the bunch was a tough-tackling, resolute performance in the intimidating surroundings of the Sükrü Saraçoglu Stadium, Istanbul, as England pipped Turkey to the head of Group Seven. Cast from a similar mould as England legend Tony Adams, John proved a redoubtable partner for Sol Campbell that night and on the strength of that performance alone should be confident of making the cut for the European Championship.

## GLEN JOHNSON

CLUB CHELSEA
BORN 23 AUGUST 1984
HEIGHT 6FT 0IN
WEIGHT 12ST
CAPS 1 (INC. 1 SUB)
GOALS 0

Glen's rise to prominence has been nothing short of meteoric. Despite spending part of the 2002/03 season on loan at Millwall, the Londoner established himself in the West Ham United first team by the end of the campaign. A £6 million summertime move to Chelsea ensued and the full-back has since gained valuable Premiership and Champions League experience to add to his seven Under-21 international caps. It's testament to Glen's talent that he plays regularly for Chelsea's all-star team. However, Euro 2004 may have come a little early for a player who has yet to appear in a competitive match at international level.

## DANNY MILLS

CLUB MIDDLESBROUGH (ON LOAN FROM LEEDS UNITED)
BORN 18 MAY 1977
HEIGHT 5FT 11IN
WEIGHT 12ST 6LB
CAPS 18 (INC. 7 SUB)
GOALS 0

Danny was one of the surprise packages of England's largely impressive 2002 World Cup campaign. Benefiting from Gary Neville's absence through injury, the former Charlton defender delivered a series of competent performances at right-back. Although he is likely to remain in Neville's shadow for the immediate future, Danny's versatility, pace and tireless application make him a valuable squad member. And unlike some of the other pretenders to the right-back berth, Danny boasts invaluable international tournament experience. Euro 2004 should be a breath of fresh air after a rather unsettled club season.

## GARY NEVILLE

CLUB MANCHESTER UNITED
BORN 18 FEBRUARY 1975
HEIGHT 5FT 11IN
WEIGHT 12ST 4LB
CAPS 62
GOALS 0

Only his best friend and skipper David Beckham is more experienced at international level than the Manchester United full-back. Gary was first called into the England fold by Terry Venables in the summer of 1995 and has been a fixture ever since. Successive managers have recognised his consistency, speed and determination and placed their faith in him. Gary's ability to organise and his vocal presence are also major assets in a relatively young England side. Despite missing the last World Cup because of a foot injury, Gary has as much tournament know-how as anyone in the squad after appearing at Euro '96, World Cup '98 and Euro 2000.

## MATTHEW UPSON

CLUB BIRMINGHAM CITY
BORN 18 APRIL 1979
HEIGHT 6FT 1IN
WEIGHT 11ST 4LB
CAPS 6
GOALS 0

What a difference a change of scene makes. After failing to hold down a regular first-team place at Arsenal, Matthew switched to Birmingham City in January 2003. And he hasn't looked back since. Matthew's progress has been so impressive that just five months after moving to the Midlands club he received an England call from Sven, making his debut as a substitute against South Africa in May. Full appearances in the qualifier victories over Slovakia and Liechtenstein followed and Upson now has a good chance of making the grade for Portugal 2004.

# MIDFIELDERS

## DAVID BECKHAM

CLUB REAL MADRID
BORN 2 MAY 1975
HEIGHT 6FT
WEIGHT 11ST 13LB
CAPS 65
GOALS 13

The inspirational skipper par excellence, David's contribution to England's Euro qualifying cause was immense. His five goals in seven qualifiers were crucial to the success of England's campaign and his work-rate and passion for the cause set the benchmark for the rest of the team. Euro 2004 will be the Real Madrid midfielder's fourth international tournament, and his second as captain. Hopefully, unlike at World Cup 2002, Becks should be 100 per cent fit this time. It is the mark of a great player to be able to deliver a tournament-winning series of displays and David is well capable of doing so in Portugal.

## NICKY BUTT

CLUB MANCHESTER UNITED
BORN 21 JANUARY 1975
HEIGHT 5FT 10IN
WEIGHT 11ST 11LB
CAPS 31
GOALS 0

Nicky has often found himself in a strange situation over the past season. While he is first choice in England's midfield, he doesn't always get a game for his club, Manchester United. Sven will be hoping this means Butt's legs are as fresh as they were at the World Cup, where he combined defensive midfield prowess with visionary passing. The Manchester-born enforcer's ability to break up opposition attacks allows team-mates Beckham, Scholes and Gerrard to roam forward with such menace.

## JOE COLE

CLUB CHELSEA
BORN 18 NOVEMBER 1981
HEIGHT 5FT 7IN
WEIGHT 9ST 8LB
CAPS 13
GOALS 2

The exciting young Chelsea midfielder is one of the richest talents available to Sven-Goran Eriksson. Cole combines purpose and poise with a sharp eye for goal and that rare ability to dribble past opponents. However, his tournament seems likely to follow the blueprint of his previous England appearances: he will be used sparingly from the bench. Unless Joe can convince the coach otherwise, inexperience may count against him in the final analysis. But it would be a brave punter who bets against the swashbuckling midfielder making telling contributions as a substitute.

## PAUL SCHOLES

CLUB MANCHESTER UNITED
BORN 16 NOVEMBER 1974
HEIGHT 5FT 7IN
WEIGHT 11ST
CAPS 59 (INC. 2 SUB)
GOALS 13

The flame-haired midfielder's importance to the team is evidenced by how rarely he is on the bench. But it is one of football's strange anomalies that a player so prolific in the early part of his England career has not scored an international goal since June 2001. However, Sven has often deployed Scholes in a deeper role of late, which partly explains his goal drought. And Paul's record in major tournaments is a good one. Expect him to get back on the scoresheet and make a major impact.

## OWEN HARGREAVES

CLUB BAYERN MUNICH
BORN 20 JANUARY 1981
HEIGHT 5FT 9IN
WEIGHT 11ST 7LB
CAPS 15 (INC. 9 SUB)
GOALS 0

As a team and a nation, England have yet to witness the best of Owen Hargreaves. Canadian-born of English parents, the energetic midfielder was, at just 21, an outstanding member of Bayern Munich's 2001 European Cup-winning team. Still, he has enjoyed relatively few opportunities for his country despite appearing at the World Cup. An ability to play several midfield defensive positions, as well as his combative nature, should see that change sooner rather than later. But, for the time being, Owen will probably have to content himself with a supporting role.

## PHILIP NEVILLE

CLUB MANCHESTER UNITED
BORN 21 JANUARY 1977
HEIGHT 5FT 11IN
WEIGHT 12ST
CAPS 44 (INC. 15 SUB)
GOALS 0

How the younger Neville's career has been transformed since that gut-wrenching moment when he conceded the penalty that saw England eliminated from Euro 2000. His metamorphosis from left-back to confident, take-no-prisoners midfielder for club and country has defied the critics and won Phil many admirers. Given his experience and versatility, the Bury-born midfielder – and he genuinely is a midfielder now – is certain to make Sven's final 23. He will provide healthy competition and invaluable cover for Manchester United colleague Nicky Butt in the crucial defensive midfield role.

## JERMAINE JENAS

CLUB NEWCASTLE UNITED
BORN 18 FEBRUARY 1983
HEIGHT 5FT 10IN
WEIGHT 12ST
CAPS 4 (INC. 4 SUB)
GOALS 0

Surely an England star of the future, the Newcastle midfielder has every chance of gaining crucial experience on the trip to Portugal. Although he is unlikely to start any games at the tournament, Jermaine's accurate passing and vibrant approach have already alerted Sven to his long-term potential. After graduating from the Under-21s, Jenas made his England debut against Australia in February 2003. Just a year earlier, he became the country's second most expensive teenager when he signed for Newcastle United from Nottingham Forest for a whopping £5 million.

## FRANK LAMPARD

CLUB CHELSEA
BORN 20 JUNE 1978
HEIGHT 6FT
WEIGHT 12ST 4LB
CAPS 16
GOALS 1

Anybody who can hold down a regular first-team spot at Chelsea, given the multi-million-pound influx of talent last

OWEN

summer, is a player to be reckoned with. Frank may not have the global reputation of some of his much-vaunted Stamford Bridge colleagues, but that has not deterred him from becoming one of the outstanding midfield talents in the Premiership. Sven has been quick to acknowledge Lampard's fine blend of energy, composure and competitive edge. The former West Ham midfielder will push hard for a place in the starting 11 in Portugal.

## DANNY MURPHY

CLUB LIVERPOOL
BORN 18 MARCH 1977
HEIGHT 5FT 9IN
WEIGHT 12ST 8LB
CAPS 9 (INC. 8 SUB)
GOALS 1

For all his neat passing and midfield industry, Danny has yet to make a real breakthrough at international level. Granted, he bagged his first England goal in a friendly against Paraguay in 2002, but his opportunities have been limited to substitute cameo appearances. Even so, there could well be a place in Sven's squad for a player who has developed a happy habit of scoring important goals for his club and whose commitment and dedication remain unquestioned. Having found greater consistency recently, the former Crewe Alexandra midfielder wouldn't let England down.

## KIERON DYER

CLUB NEWCASTLE UNITED
BORN 29 DECEMBER 1978
HEIGHT 5FT 7IN
WEIGHT 10ST 1LB
CAPS 19 (INC. 12 SUB)
GOALS 0

Kieron's international career has often been interrupted by injury. The gifted Newcastle midfielder made his England debut under Kevin Keegan back in September 1999. But he has made only a handful of starts since. Likely to be used in short bursts as he was at the 2002 World Cup, Dyer will be desperate to make an impression after hovering around the fringes for so long. Under the direction of former England boss Sir Bobby Robson, Kieron has developed a fine range of passing to complement his lung-busting industry.

## STEVEN GERRARD

CLUB LIVERPOOL
BORN 30 MAY 1980
HEIGHT 6FT 1IN
WEIGHT 12ST 3LB
CAPS 21 (INC. 1 SUB)
GOALS 3

Gerrard is without question one of the superstars of this England side. The Liverpool midfielder has also become something of a talisman. In the 20 friendly and competitive appearances that followed his winning debut in May 2000, England have never lost. However, Steven's participation in major tournaments has been limited (mainly by injury) to a single substitute appearance at Euro 2000. If Sven's men are to achieve European glory in Portugal, it is essential Gerrard remains fit. Any team would miss his combativeness, energy and dogged determination. A key player for England.

## SCOTT PARKER

CLUB CHELSEA
BORN 13 OCTOBER 1980
HEIGHT 5FT 7IN
WEIGHT 11ST 1LB
CAPS 1 (INC. 1 SUB)
GOALS 0

Technically-gifted, an excellent passer and a real hard worker, it's no wonder that the 23-year old was so coveted by big-spending Chelsea. It shows Scott's ambition that he was prepared to make the move from a Charlton side where he was guaranteed a first-team place, to star-studded Chelsea where competition for places is much more fierce. "You've always got to push yourself as a player," says Scott. "When I first joined up with England, it was nerve-racking being there with the likes of Beckham and Scholes, but I came away hungry for more."

# FORWARDS

## EMILE HESKEY

CLUB LIVERPOOL
BORN 11 JANUARY 1978
HEIGHT 6FT 1IN
WEIGHT 14ST 4LB
CAPS 38
GOALS 5

England will be hoping Emile can play with genuine purpose in Portugal. When focused on using his strength and pace, the former Leicester front-man is a genuine handful for defenders. Sven clearly appreciates the unselfish, workmanlike approach Heskey offers and has often placed his faith in the Liverpool man. Still, given the emergence of Wayne Rooney and the continued goalscoring excellence of Michael Owen, Emile must fight to make the starting line-up in Portugal. If he could just deliver more goals, his participation at the tournament would be virtually guaranteed.

## WAYNE ROONEY

CLUB EVERTON
BORN 24 OCTOBER 1985
HEIGHT 5FT 10IN
WEIGHT 12ST 4LB
CAPS 9
GOALS 3

Not since Paul Gascoigne took the 1990 World Cup by storm has there been so much excitement about an England player. Wayne's precocious talent – a magnificent blend of skill, pace and strength – saw him become England's youngest-ever goalscorer at the tender age of 17 years and 317 days. The Everton attacker will still only be 18 when Euro 2004 kicks off, but he possesses a wonderfully mature football brain. It may be tempting fate to say so, but England have unearthed a genuine match-winner in the precocious Liverpudlian.

## DARIUS VASSELL

CLUB ASTON VILLA
BORN 13 JUNE 1980
HEIGHT 5FT 7IN
WEIGHT 12ST
CAPS 15 (INC. 10 SUB)
GOALS 4

It is an oddity that Darius Vassell remains more convincing in the dizzy heights of international football than he does in the Premiership. Four goals in just five starts for England represents an excellent return. Darius cut his teeth at Under-21 level before breaking into the senior squad in early 2002. His pace and sharp movement were genuine assets for England at the World Cup. Yet his most telling intervention was the predatory, deadlock-breaking strike that set England on the path to victory over Turkey in the Euro qualifiers.

## MICHAEL OWEN

CLUB LIVERPOOL
BORN 14 DECEMBER 1979
HEIGHT 5FT 8IN
WEIGHT 10ST 13LB
CAPS 53 (INC. 10 SUB)
GOALS 24

Yet again Owen will shoulder the burden of goalscoring responsibility at a major tournament. With a strike rate of a goal almost every other game, it is little wonder so much is expected of the Liverpool striker. Michael rose to international prominence as a teenager with some inspired performances and one particularly spectacular goal at the 1998 World Cup. A key figure in England's qualifying campaign, he weighed in with five vital goals. Owen usually rises to the occasion and must be at his best for England to taste glory.

## JAMES BEATTIE

CLUB SOUTHAMPTON
BORN 27 FEBRUARY 1978
HEIGHT 6FT 1IN
WEIGHT 13ST 6LB
CAPS 5
GOALS 0

Despite several prolific seasons with Southampton, James has had few opportunities to establish himself as a regular for England. He has yet to break his international duck in the handful of appearances he has been granted since making his debut against Australia in February 2003. James' immense aerial strength would give Sven another option in Portugal and, in the long-term, Beattie would surely benefit from David Beckham's expert delivery. If James can maintain his consistency at club level, you sense his time will come for England. But maybe not quite yet.

## THE HOPEFULS

AT NEARLY EVERY MAJOR TOURNAMENT, there are late arrivals whose influence on proceedings is memorable. While Tottenham's **Darren Anderton** is unlikely to make his customary late run into the squad, there are other players in that team who might just make the cut. **Ledley King** has impressed in his limited outings, particularly with his goal against Portugal in his full debut, and there are plenty of other central defenders who will harbour hopes of a call. Among them is Manchester United's **Wes Brown**, an outstanding athlete whose opportunities have been limited by injury.

**Anthony Gardner**, another Spurs defender, has cause for optimism after being drafted into the squad for the friendly against Denmark in November. Celtic's **Chris Sutton** has also been admirably consistent when deployed in central defence by Martin O'Neill this term, but he seems to have closed the door on a return to the international fold.

Leading the outsiders vying for one of the few midfield places not sewn up in advance are Fulham's **Sean Davis**, **David Dunn** of Birmingham City and Manchester City's **Steve McManaman**. After a successful transition from Blackburn Rovers to the Midlands last summer, Dunn looks the man most likely of the trio.

Meanwhile, **Alan Thompson**, of Celtic, or Aston Villa's **Gareth Barry** could force their way into Sven's thinking because they operate on the left side of midfield, so often a problem area for England in the past.

A good haul of goals in the last months of the season might see **Jermain Defoe** of Spurs called into the squad. But you sense Manchester City's **Robbie Fowler** and **Kevin Phillips** of Southampton would have to produce something special to show they can still cut it at international level.

And whoever holds on to Everton's number one jersey out of **Nigel Martyn** and **Richard Wright** could prove he has the pedigree to challenge for the third goalkeeping spot.

***NB. Player statistics were correct at January 1, 2004.***

## PICTURE CREDITS

The publishers would like to thank the following sources for their kind permission to reproduce the pictures in this book:

**Action Images**/18, 50, 58.

**AFP/GettyImages**/Stringer 69mt, 69mb.

**Empics** /Matthew Ashton 5bl, 32, 48; /Adam Davy 33, 39, 47, 73; /Mark Earthy 42; /Mike Egerton 44; /Nigel French 20, 34; /Laurence Graffith 4, 5, 16, 50, 51; /Christian Liewig 36, 52-3; /Tony Marshall 43, 45, 46, 49, 62; /Peter Robinson 5, 63; /Neal Simpson 27, 35, 38; /Agencia Ferique 69t, 69b.

**FAOPL** 1-2, 2-3, 6bl, 7, 8, 9, 10, 11, 12tl, 12-3, 15, 17, 22, 26, 29, 37, 56, 60-1, 61, 64, 71, 75, 76. 78, 80.

**Portuguese Tourist Office/London** 66, 67, 68

**Topham Picturepoint** 19.

Every effort has been made to acknowledge correctly and contact the source and/or copyright holder of each picture, and Carlton Books Limited apologises for any unintentional errors or omissions which will be corrected in future editions of this book.